Shakespeare

and the Art of

Verbal Seduction

Shakespeare

and the Art of

Verbal Seduction

Wayne F. Hill and Cynthia J. Öttchen

GRAMERCY BOOKS
NEW YORK

This 2006 edition is published by Gramercy Books, an imprint of Random House Value Publishing, by arrangement with Three Rivers Press, member of the Crown Publishing Group, divisions of Random House, Inc., New York.

Gramercy is a registered trademark and the colophon is a trademark of Random House, Inc.

Random House
New York • Toronto • London • Sydney • Auckland
www.randomhouse.com

Design by Maggie Hinders

Printed and bound in the United States of America.

Library of Congress Cataloging-in-Publication Data

Shakespeare, William, 1564-1616.
    Shakespeare and the art of verbal seduction / [edited by] Wayne F. Hill and Cynthia J. Öttchen.
        p. cm.
    Originally published: New York : Three Rivers Press, c2003.
    ISBN-13: 978-0-517-22806-7
    ISBN-10: 0-517-22806-8
        1. Shakespeare, William, 1564-1616—Quotations. 2. Seduction—Quotations, maxims, etc. I. Hill, Wayne F. II. Öttchen, Cynthia J. III. Title.

PR2771.H55 2006
822.3'3—dc22

2005055084

10 9 8 7 6 5 4 3 2 1

He, he, and you, and you, my liege, and I,

Are pick-purses in love, and we deserve to die.

LOVE'S LABOUR'S LOST

Contents

ACKNOWLEDGMENTS

MANY PEOPLE helped make this book possible. For making it happen, we would like to thank Lauren Shakely at Random House and Jonathan Lloyd and Tara Wynne at Curtis Brown. And thanks to Random House's Lance Troxel for his sure but light touch.

Thank you, Miguel Cutillas, for designing the cover illustration.

Thanks also to Anne Berkeley, Andre Mangeot, and Andrea Porter for bemused assistance in sorting extracts. Thank you, Emily Dening, for preparing the manuscripts.

Finally we thank all the readers and abusers of *Shakespeare's Insults, Educating Your Wit*, who wrote and insisted on an encore. We just happened to have a little something for your twisted imaginations. Write to us about this.

How to Handle This Book

Everybody wants to be seduced. And at the same time, everyone's trying to do it. Seduction is a universal dream that hardly anyone makes an intimate reality. Where is the deft touch, that perfect word people long for? Seduction is the most played—and worst played—game in human history. So few people win that the laurels languish.

Winners have to be wonderful with words. The person you desire will be ready for you if you say what they're ready to hear—what they're deep down dying to be told. The bad lines and the groans are a crying shame. For everyone's mutual pleasure, and a global increase in satisfaction, we bring in Shakespeare, the greatest player of all time. He enters as never before, revealing in bare, exciting variety how he makes his language come together. We are directors, and this is a play. Together we'll make his voice yours.

We have already collected his insults, pure dramatic conflict distilled into stunning little economies of words. Now we gather up the language of forging connections and bringing people together. And again he creates whole worlds in brief verbal twists. What we're after is how the master uses language. Not to explain it, but to show it. If he knows the human heart so well, what does he do to join two people, to arrive at a yes? We want those little energetics of language.

We choose to lift them out of context. It doesn't matter now who said what to whom. It's Shakespeare's gift with words we want unwrapped. We leave it to you to supply the people to say them and play them on, yourself being one. The lines between these covers weren't all created for helping people into love, but all these persuasive sentences might work for love.

The myriad shapes of this seductive language serve the mercurial needs of a love affair. We've let them find their way into ten chapters, from first encounter through all the barriers to passion and finishing with lines that render boredom most unlikely. What could be more useful? Who could be more helpful? Our chapter introductions are more like intermission entertainments than sober commentaries. Appropriate to seduction, we're playing, not saying.

Most of the time the extracts come straight from the page. But to make lines useful for direct address, we say things like "[I'll] out-tongue [your] complaints," rather than the congested correctness of "My services which I have done the signiory,/ Shall out-tongue his complaints." When we've tweaked, we make it obvious with ellipses ... and [square brackets]. We make sure subject and verb still agree. When it's essential, we clear away just enough clinging bits of context so, instead of quoting scraps of other Shakespearean characters, you and he and we make a character out of you.

Go on. Slip into the pages; form the sounds in your mouth; play upon the words. Get the feel for rhythm and tone. Watch the language transform before your eyes from words into images, ideas, and emotions. A sexy new sensibility will energize your entrances and exits. You may develop style. You might even succeed at seduction. You'll certainly re-create yourself as a more interesting character. Arouse interest in yourself. Imply wider riches. No need to quote slavishly verbatim: Shakespeare calls for drama, not automata. Get ready to expend new reserves of verbal energy and get somewhere with the creature you desire.

Shakespeare

and the Art of

Verbal Seduction

Ice-breaking

Everyone is a stranger, including you, and Shakespeare does something about it. He creates perfect openers.

When complicated people bump into each other, it's the delicate drama of the first impression. It's pure comedy, if not pure tragedy, fantasy, or history. Which is why it's pure felicity for Shakespeare to appear suddenly on the scene to sort things out. Chief among the playwrights he makes himself invisible by letting every sort of human character shine through him. He is sheer camouflage. Use his lines as sheer bricolage. Open these pages, and do it yourself.

When there was tension in the playhouse, Shakespeare got people's attention. "O for a muse of fire," he said, and into the play everybody went. Go and do likewise. Melt your audience of one. But assuming you can't come up with the perfect words at the perfect time, at least create the impression that you can. Learn to play with Shakespeare's wit and go for a happy accident.

Today's awful lines are offal, but Shakespeare keeps chat-up standards up. There's no point in reinventing genius. His down-to-earth message: Please, be discriminating. Revel in human strangerhood without ruining the neighborhood. Avoid the groans, say what succeeds. Use these certified good lines as needed, and when they run out, bow out. Retire offstage. If you think you need more, you honestly need to leave people alone.

ALL'S WELL THAT ENDS WELL

Are you meditating on virginity?

1.1.108

Now I see
The myst'ry of your loneliness.

1.3.165–66

Fair maid, send forth thine eye.

2.3.52

[You're] a fair creature.

3.6.112

They told me that your name was Fontybell.

4.2.1

ANTONY AND CLEOPATRA

Come, you'll play with me, sir?

2.5.6

How now, friend Eros?

3.5.1

Where hast thou been, my heart?

3.13.177

AS YOU LIKE IT

[You] are fair with [your] feeding.

1.1.11–12

What shall be our sport then?

1.2.29

How now Wit, whither wander you?

1.2.53–54

Your heart's desires be with you!

1.2.187

O excellent young man!

1.2.201

Gentleman, wear this for me.

1.2.236

In my voice most welcome shall you be.

2.4.85

If ladies be but young and fair,
They have the gift to know it.

2.7.37–38

Sit you down in gentleness.

2.7.124

Be blest for your good comfort.

2.7.135

Where dwell you pretty youth?

3.2.328

Are you native of this place?

3.2.331

Your accent is something finer than you could purchase
in so removed a dwelling.

3.2.333–34

[You] seem to have the quotidian of love upon [you].
3.2.356

I profess curing [love madness] by counsel.
3.2.393

Well, the gods give us joy!
3.3.41

The sight of lovers feedeth those in love.
3.4.53

Why do you look on me?
3.5.41

[I know you] not very well, but I have met [you] oft.
3.5.106

[You are] a pretty youth—not very pretty—
But sure . . . proud, and yet [your] pride becomes [you].
3.5.113–14

I prithee, pretty youth, let me be better acquainted with
thee.
4.1.1–2

My errand is to you, fair youth.
4.3.6

[You] play the swaggerer.
4.3.14

I should have been a woman.
4.3.175

I know you are a gentleman.
5.2.53

Look upon [me], love [me]. I worship you.

5.2.81

Let me have audience for a word or two.

5.4.150

CYMBELINE

[You are] the fairest that I have look'd upon.

2.4.32

Come, here's my heart.

3.4.79

By Jupiter, an angel! or, if not,
An earthly paragon! Behold divineness.

3.7.15–16

For beauty, [you make] barren the swell'd boast
Of him that best could speak.

5.5.162–63

For feature, [you] lame
The shrine of Venus.

5.5.163–64

[You are] a shop of all the qualities that man
Loves woman for.

5.5.166–67

[You are] worthy
To inlay heaven with stars.

5.5.352–53

HAMLET

What art thou that usurp'st this time of night?

1.1.49

And now, what's the news with you?

1.2.42

O fear me not.

1.3.51

Thou com'st in such a questionable shape
That I will speak to thee.

1.4.43–44

Soft, methinks I scent the morning air.

1.5.58

Hillo, ho, ho, boy. Come, bird, come.

1.5.118

Have [I] given [you] any hard words of late?

2.1.107

Buzz, buzz.

2.2.389

Come, give us a taste of your quality. Come, a passionate
speech.

2.2.427–28

[You are] th'expectancy and rose of the fair state.

3.1.154

[You are] the glass of fashion and the mould of form.

3.1.155

[You are] th'observed of all observers.

3.1.156

O *confound the rest.*

3.2.172

[I will] call you [my] mouse.

3.4.185

[You are] lov'd of the distracted multitude.

4.3.4

How do you, pretty lady?

4.5.41

O rose of May!

4.5.157

I have words to speak in thine ear.

4.6.22

Love between [us] like the palm might flourish.

5.2.40

If [you] were at leisure, I should impart a thing to you.

5.2.90–91

Methinks it is very sultry and hot for my complexion.

5.2.97–98

I pray you pass with your best violence.
I am afeard you make a wanton of me.

5.2.302–3

Love's Labour's Lost

Did I not dance with you in Brabant once?

2.1.113

Vouchsafe to show the sunshine of your face,
That we, like savages, may worship it.

5.2.201–2

White-handed mistress, one sweet word with thee.

5.2.230

One word in secret.

5.2.236

Will you vouchsafe with me to change a word?

5.2.238

One word in private with you ere I die.

5.2.254

Measure for Measure

I beseech you, . . . look in this gentleman's face.

2.1.145

Look upon [my] honour; 'tis for a good purpose.—Doth
your honour mark [my] face?

2.1.146–47

I'll be supposed upon a book, [your] face is the worst
thing about [you].

2.1.153–54

Your bum is the greatest thing about you.

2.1.214–15

What's your suit?

2.2.28

Sound a thought upon your tongue.

2.2.141

The tempter, or the tempted, who sins most, ha?

2.2.164

How now fair maid?

2.4.30

[Your] saucy sweetness . . . coins heaven's image.

2.4.45

[You] find yourself desir'd of such a person.

2.4.91

What hoa! Peace here; grace and good company!

3.1.44

A word with you.
As many as you please.

3.1.50–51

Now . . . what's the comfort?

3.1.53

Vouchsafe a word, young sister, but one word.

3.1.150–51

Might you dispense with your leisure, I would by and by
have some speech with you.

3.1.153–54

I am so out of love with life.

3.1.170–71

How doth my dear morsel, thy mistress?

3.2.52

Of whence are you?

3.2.210

Here comes a man of comfort.

4.1.8

Very well met, and well come.

4.1.26

        Millions of false eyes
Are stuck upon thee.

4.1.60–61

Happily you something know.

4.2.93–94

O, 'tis an accident that heaven provides.

4.3.76

Good morning to you, fair and gracious [woman].

4.3.111

Do you not smile at this?

5.1.165

Let's see thy face.

5.1.204

O most kind maid.

5.1.391

Joy to you.

5.1.523

The Merry Wives of Windsor

Pretty virginity!

1.1.43

By my troth, you are very well met: by your leave, good
mistress.

1.1.174–75

How now, good woman, how dost thou?

1.4.129

Pretty weathercock?

3.2.15

A Midsummer Night's Dream

How now, my love? Why is your cheek so pale?
How chance the roses there do fade so fast?

1.1.128–29

A lover, or a tyrant?

1.2.29

What angel wakes me from my flowery bed?

3.1.124

Asleep, my love?
What, dead, my dove?

5.1.311–12

MUCH ADO ABOUT NOTHING

In mine eye, [you] are the sweetest lady that ever I
　　looked on.

1.1.174–75

Lady, will you walk a bout with your friend?

2.1.79

Come, bid me do anything for thee.

4.1.287

OTHELLO

Hail to thee, lady, and the grace of heaven,
Before, behind thee, and on every hand
Enwheel thee round!

2.1.85–87

[You're] a most exquisite lady.

2.3.18

[You're] a most fresh and delicate creature.

2.3.20

What an eye [you have]! methinks it sounds a parley to
　　provocation.

2.3.21–22

[You are] indeed perfection.

2.3.25

A fine woman, a fair woman, a sweet woman!

4.1.175–76

[Your] body and beauty
unprovide my mind.

4.1.202–3

Pray, chuck, come hither.

4.2.23

Let me see your eyes.

4.2.25

[You are] like one of heaven.

4.2.37

Thou young and rose-lipped cherubin.

4.2.64

[Thou] are so lovely fair and smell'st so sweet
That the sense aches at thee.

4.2.68–69

O, these men, these men!

4.3.59

O balmy breath.

5.2.16

[You are] the sweetest innocent
That e'er did lift up eye.

5.2.197–98

PERICLES

I life would wish, and that I might
Waste it for you like taper-light.

1.Chorus.15–16

[You are] so buxom, blithe and full of face
As heaven had lent [you] all his grace.
                                    1.Chorus.23–24

[Your] face [is] the book of praises, where is read
Nothing but curious pleasures.
                                    1.1.16–17

[Mine] eye presumes to reach.
                                    1.1.33–34

I bequeath a happy peace to you.
                                    1.1.51

Here pleasures court mine eyes.
                                    1.2.7

Thou hast mov'd [me]; what seest thou in [my] looks?
                                    1.2.52

[Your] face was to mine eye beyond all wonder.
                                    1.2.75

        Feast here awhile,
Until our stars that frown lend us a smile.
                                    1.4.107–8

[You] sit here like Beauty's child, whom Nature gat
For men to see, and seeing wonder at.
                                    2.2.6–7

Sure [you're] a gallant gentleman.
                                    2.3.32

[You're] as a fair day in summer, wondrous fair.
                                    2.5.36

Look how fresh she looks!

3.2.81

[Your] excellent complexion . . . did steal
The eyes of young and old.

4.1.40–41

Why lament you pretty one?

4.2.64

I think that I shall have something to do with you.

4.2.82–83

Pray you, come hither awhile.

4.2.114

You have fortunes coming upon you.

4.2.114–15

Come, young one, I like the manner of your garments
well.

4.2.131–32

None would look on [any other],
But cast their gazes on [your] face.

4.3.32–33

Your ears unto your eyes I'll reconcile.

4.4.22

How now, wholesome iniquity.

4.6.23–24

Have you that a man may deal withal, and defy the
surgeon?

4.6.24–25

[You] sing like one immortal, and [you] dance
As goddess-like.

5.Chorus.3–4

What is [my] will?
That [you] have [yours].

5.1.5–6

[You are] all happy as the fairest of all.

5.1.48

      Prithee speak;
Falseness cannot come from thee, for thou look'st
Modest as Justice, and thou seem'st a palace
For the crown'd Truth to dwell in.

5.1.119–22

Thou look'st like one I lov'd indeed.

5.1.124–25

Thou dost look
Like Patience gazing on kings' graves, and smiling
Extremity out of act.

5.1.137–39

Are you flesh and blood?
Have you a working pulse, and are no fairy
Motion? Well, speak on. Where were you born?

5.1.152–54

Romeo and Juliet

I pray come and crush a cup of wine.

1.2.82

One fairer than my love! The all-seeing sun
Ne'er saw [your] match since first the world begun.
                                  1.2.94–95

God be with [your] soul,
[You're] a merry man.
                                  1.3.39–40

Thou wast the prettiest babe that e'er I [saw].
                                  1.3.60

Summer hath not such a flower [as you].
                                  1.3.77

[You're] a flower, in faith a very flower.
                                  1.3.78

[I] read o'er the volume of [your] face
And find delight writ there with beauty's pen.
                                  1.3.81–82

[You] precious book of love, [you] unbound lover,
To beautify [you] only lacks a cover.
                                  1.3.87–88

I'll look to like, if looking liking move.
                                  1.3.97

[Your] beauty [is] too rich for use, for earth too dear.
                                  1.5.46

[You are] a snowy dove trooping with crows.
                                  1.5.47

I am too bold.
                                  2.2.14

What man art thou that thus bescreen'd in night
So stumblest on my counsel?

2.2.52–53

What a man are you?

2.4.113

[I am a man] that God hath made, himself to mar.

2.4.114–15

[I] know not how to choose a man.

2.5.38–39

I'll warrant [you] as gentle as a lamb.

2.5.44

Did ever dragon keep so fair a cave?

3.2.74

[You dwell] in mortal paradise of such sweet flesh.

3.2.82

Heaven is here where [you] live.

3.3.29–30

Art thou a man? Thy form cries out thou art.

3.3.108

Thou hast amaz'd me.

3.3.113

Heaven and earth . . . do meet in thee at once.

3.3.119–20

How is't, my soul? Let's talk.

3.5.25

[You are] the sweetest flower of all the field.
4.5.29

[You are] the dearest morsel of the earth.
5.3.46

[Your] beauty makes
This vault a feasting presence, full of light.
5.3.85–86

THE TAMING OF THE SHREW

Think you a little din can daunt mine ears?
1.2.198

Where did you study all this goodly speech?
2.1.256

Come, where be these gallants? Who's at home?
3.2.84

THE TEMPEST

What cheer?
1.1.2

Heigh, my hearts! cheerly, cheerly, my hearts!
1.1.5

Fine apparition! My quaint [nymph],
Hark in thine ear.
1.2.319–20

I have followed [your music],
Or it hath drawn me rather.

                                        1.2.396–97

        My prime request,
Which I do last pronounce, is, O you wonder!
If you be maid or no?

                                        1.2.428–31

[This place] was never grac'd before with such a
    paragon.

                                        2.1.70–71

[Your] word is more than the miraculous harp.

                                        2.1.83

[You are] the rarest that e'er came [here].

                                        2.1.95

Hast thou not dropp'd from heaven?

                                        2.2.137

[You] make a wonder of a poor drunkard!

                                        2.2.165–66

Alas now, pray you, work not so hard.

                                        3.1.15–16

Pray, set it down, and rest you.

                                        3.1.17

I do beseech you—
Chiefly that I might set it in my prayers—
What is your name?

                                        3.1.34–36

What harmony is this?

3.3.18

Now I will believe that there are unicorns.

3.3.21–22

Sit, then, and talk with [me].

4.1.32

[I am] spell-stopped.

5.1.61

O, wonder!
How many goodly creatures are there here!

5.1.181–82

O brave new world,
That has such people in 't!

5.1.183–84

Please you, draw near.

5.1.317

Gentle breath of yours my sails
Must fill, or else my project fails,
Which was to please.

Epilogue.11–13

TROILUS AND CRESSIDA

Do you know a man if you see him?

1.2.64–65

What sneaking fellow comes yonder?

1.2.229

O admirable youth!

1.2.238

O admirable man!

1.2.241

What too curious dreg espies my sweet lady in the
fountain of our love?

3.2.64–65

TWELFTH NIGHT

There is a fair behaviour in thee, Captain.

1.2.47

I am sure care's an enemy to life.

1.3.2–3

Bless you, fair shrew.

1.3.46

Good Mistress Accost, I desire better acquaintance.

1.3.51–52

Shall we set about some revels?

1.3.133–34

Are you a comedian?

1.5.183

What is your parentage?

1.5.281

What is your name?

3.1.98

I come to whet your gentle thoughts.

3.1.107

What's to do?
Shall we go see the relics of this town?

3.3.18–19

Sweet Lady, ho, ho!

3.4.17

Sad, lady? I could be sad.

3.4.19

God comfort thee! Why dost thou smile so, and kiss thy
    hand so oft?

3.4.32–33

Why, this is very midsummer madness.

3.4.55

Talkest thou nothing but of ladies?

4.2.27

THE TWO GENTLEMEN OF VERONA

All happiness bechance to thee.

1.1.61

I would I knew [your] mind.

1.2.33

Ay, madam, you may say what sights you see;
I see things too, although you judge I wink.

1.2.138–39

[I am] she that you gaze on so, as she sits at supper.
2.1.42

[You are] not so fair . . . as well-favoured.
2.1.48

Madam and mistress, a thousand good-morrows.
2.1.91

O, 'give-ye-good-ev'n! Here's a million of manners.
2.1.92–93

Though the chameleon Love can feed on the air, I am
    one that am nourished by my victuals; and would fain
    have meat.
2.1.162–64

[Your] worth is warrant for [your] welcome hither.
2.4.97

Sweet lady, entertain [me].
2.4.99

[You have] a sweet mouth.
3.1.321

[You are] a virtuous gentlewoman, mild, and beautiful.
4.4.178

Black men are pearls in beauteous ladies' eyes.
5.2.12

Vouchsafe me for my meed but one fair look;
A smaller boon than this I cannot beg,
And less than this I am sure you cannot give.
5.4.23–25

THE WINTER'S TALE

Tongue-tied our queen? speak you.

1.2.27

My prisoner? or my guest?

1.2.54–55

What! hast smutch'd thy nose?

1.2.121

　　　Mine honest friend,
Will you take eggs for money?

1.2.160–61

　　　If you would seek us,
We are yours i'th' garden: shall's attend you there?

1.2.177–78

How now, boy?

1.2.207

What is this? sport?

2.1.58

Follow me girls.

4.4.314

Angling

SHAKESPEARE is nothing if not charming, while you undoubtedly lean slightly more toward the nothing. But hope abounds. You can be as amusing as he is. Exactly as amusing: cast his lines.

Shakespeare knows how to create charm out of nothing but words. He sinks good lines into plots, thereby allowing relationships to grow. We do it by taking them out of plots and casting them into a timeline of seduction. Why? So you can *make time* by playing with his lines. Shakespeare always gives good line.

I am angling now
Though you perceive me not how I give line.

His funny, interesting gobbets of charm are the everyday way to get the hang of what you can get away with in your seductions. Find out who's receptive to what. Here are words people will want to nibble at, to steal love's sweet bait from fearful hooks. The angler with the most appealing bait eventually lands the fattest and most appreciative fish. Let that angler be you.

In all this babbling badinage you never know what lurks and darts below the surface. But what lurks rises, what rises strikes, what strikes bites, and what bites is caught. Keep casting into the riffle. Words beyond mere prosaic reach will lure them up. The one you desire desires shimmer and flash, wants reasons to respond. The one you want wants to feel singled out, to leap laughing, make a splash. So tickle, tempt, and tease them into your net. Take the time it takes to reel in something real. Shakespeare's bits are the baits, the beautifully tied flies.

All's Well That Ends Well

Now, fair one, does your business follow us?

2.1.98

Antony and Cleopatra

Am I not an inch of fortune better than she?

1.2.60

If you were but an inch of fortune better than I, where
would you choose it?

1.2.61–62

Give me some music—music, moody food
Of us that trade in love.

2.4.1–2

You shall hear from me still. The time shall not
Outgo my thinking on you.

3.2.60–61

[You're] very knowing;
I do perceiv't.

3.3.23–24

I have eyes upon [you];
And [your] affairs come to me on the wind.

3.6.63–64

As You Like It

From henceforth I will . . . devise sports. Let me see,
what think you of falling in love?

1.2.23–24

Young gentleman, your spirits are too bold for your
  years.
1.2.162–63

Young sir; your reputation shall not . . . be misprized.
1.2.169–70

I would I were invisible, to catch the strong fellow by
  the leg.
1.2.199–200

Fare thee well, thou art a gallant youth.
1.2.218

Thy words are too precious to be cast away upon curs.
  Throw some of them at me; come lame me with
  reasons.
1.3.4–6

Let us talk in good earnest. Is it possible, on such a
  sudden, you should fall into so strong a liking?
1.3.24–25

    This shepherd's passion
Is much upon my fashion.
2.4.57–58

Live a little, comfort a little, cheer thyself a little.
2.6.5

Well said! Thou lookst cheerly, and I'll be with thee
  quickly.
2.6.13–14

    What a life is this,
That your poor friends must woo your company.
2.7.9–10

Give me your hand
And let me all your fortunes understand.
                              2.7.202–3

Thou thrice-crowned queen of night, survey
Thy huntress' name, that my full life doth sway.
                              3.2.2–4

O ominous! [you] come to kill my heart!
                              3.2.242

Do you not know I am a woman? When I think, I must
    speak.
                              3.2.245–46

[You are] just as high as my heart.
                              3.2.264

You are full of pretty answers.
                              3.2.265

You have a nimble wit.
                              3.2.271

The worst fault you have is to be in love.
                              3.2.277

[Being in love] 'tis a fault I will not change for your best
    virtue.
                              3.2.278

I'll tarry no longer with you. Farewell good Signior Love.
                              3.2.286–87

Thank God I am not a woman, to be touched with so
    many giddy offences as he hath generally taxed their
    whole sex withal.

$$3.2.339-42$$

Fancy-monger.

$$3.2.354-55$$

He taught me how to know a man in love; in which cage
    of rushes I am sure you are not prisoner.

$$3.2.359-61$$

Imagine me [your] love, [your] mistress; and . . . every
    day woo me.

$$3.2.395-97$$

I will take upon me to wash your liver as clean as a
    sound sheep's heart, that there shall not be one spot
    of love in't.

$$3.2.410-12$$

I would not be cured [of love], youth.

$$3.2.413$$

Come every day to my cote and woo me.

$$3.2.415$$

And by the way, you shall tell me where in the forest you
    live.

$$3.2.419$$

Am I the man yet?

$$3.3.2-3$$

Doth my simple feature content you?

$$3.3.3$$

The forehead of a married man is more honourable than
the bare brow of a bachelor.

> 3.3.53-55

[You] ask me of what parentage I [am]: I [tell you] of as
good as [you].

> 3.4.32-33

Laugh and let me go.

> 3.4.33-34

O that's a brave man! [You] write brave verses, speak
brave words, swear brave oaths, and break them
bravely, quite traverse, athwart the heart of [your]
lover.

> 3.4.36-39

I'll prove a busy actor in [your] play.

> 3.4.55

> Mine eyes,
Which I have darted at thee, hurt thee not.

> 3.5.24-25

I am sure, there is no force in eyes
That can do hurt.

> 3.5.26-27

You insult, exult and all at once.

> 3.5.36

> 'Od's my little life,
I think [you] mean to tangle my eyes too!

> 3.5.43-44

'Tis not your inky brows, your black silk hair,
Your bugle eyeballs, nor your cheek of cream
That can entame my spirits to your worship.
3.5.46–48

You are a thousand times a properer man
Than she a woman.

3.5.51–52

Sweet youth, I pray you chide a year together.
I had rather hear you chide than this man woo.
3.5.64–65

Who ever lov'd that lov'd not at first sight?
3.5.82

[You're] but a peevish boy—yet [you] talk well—
But what care I for words?

3.5.110–11

Words do well
When he that speaks them pleases those that hear.
3.5.111–12

The poor world is almost six thousand years old, and in
all this time there was not any man died in his own
person . . . in a love-cause.
4.1.89–92

Men have died from time to time and worms have eaten
them, but not for love.

4.1.101–3

An eye may profit by a tongue.

4.3.83

Is't possible, that on so little acquaintance you should
    like [me]? That but seeing, you should love [me]?
    And loving woo? And wooing, [I] should grant?
                                        5.2.1–4

Wounded [is my heart] . . . with the eyes of a lady.
                                        5.2.24

I like [you] very well.

                                        5.4.53

You and [I] are sure together,
As the winter to foul weather.

                                        5.4.134–35

CYMBELINE

I am bound to wonder.

                                        1.7.81

        [I wish I possessed] this object, which
Takes prisoner of the wild motion of mine eye,
Firing it only here.

                                        1.7.102–4

Good morrow, fairest: . . . your sweet hand.
                                        2.3.85

                    Boy,
Thou hast look'd thyself into my grace,
And art mine own.

                                        5.5.93–95

Walk with me: speak freely.

                                        5.5.119

HAMLET

'Tis but our fantasy,
And will not let belief take hold.

1.1.26–27

Is not this something more than fantasy?

1.1.57

Bend you to remain
Here in the cheer and comfort of [my] eye.

1.2.115–16

Thou . . . spirit of health . . .
Bring with thee airs from heaven.

1.4.40–41

Go on, I'll follow thee.

1.4.79

Adieu, adieu, adieu. Remember me.

1.5.91

[You] very wild,
Addicted so and so.

2.1.18–19

[I] fall to such perusal of [thy] face
As [I] would draw it.

2.1.90–91

Good gentleman, [all have] much talk'd of you.

2.2.19

Madam, I swear I use no art at all.

2.2.96

Good madam, stay awhile, I will be faithful.

2.2.114

What do you think of me?

2.2.129

     I had seen this hot love on the wing—
As I perceiv'd it, I must tell you.

2.2.132–33

     What would [you] do
Had [you] the motive and the cue for passion
That I have?

2.2.554–56

     The devil hath power
T'assume a pleasing shape.

2.2.595–96

'Tis now the very witching time of night.

3.2.379

Thou turn'st my eyes into my very soul.

3.4.89

One word more, good lady.

3.4.182

     [I] hear
There's tricks i'th' world.

4.5.4–5

Why, now you speak
Like a good child and a true gentleman.

4.5.147–48

Sweets to the sweet.

5.1.236

Speak feelingly.

5.2.109

This pearl is thine.
Here's to thy health.

5.2.284–85

[I] carouse to thy fortune.

5.2.292

LOVE'S LABOUR'S LOST

I do betray myself with blushing.

1.2.124

Fair weather after you!

1.2.135

Lady, I will commend you to mine own heart.

1.2.179

Sweet health and fair desires consort your grace!

2.1.177

Thy own wish wish I thee in every place!

2.2.178

If you deny to dance, let's hold more chat.

5.2.228

MEASURE FOR MEASURE

In [your] youth
There is a prone and speechless dialect
Such as move men.

1.2.172–74

It is a man's voice!

1.4.7

The jewel that we find, we stoop and take't,
Because we see it.

2.1.24–25

I am at war 'twixt will and will not.

2.2.32–33

[You] speak, and 'tis such sense
That my sense breeds with it.

2.2.142–43

Now you are come, you will be gone.

3.1.175

You are pleasant, sir, and speak apace.

3.2.109

I can do you little harm.

3.2.161

Bliss and goodness on you!

3.2.209

Leave [I you] to [your] events, with a prayer they may
    prove prosperous.

3.2.231–33

Let me excuse me, and believe me so.
4.1.12

My mirth [you] much displease, but please my woe.
4.1.13

My most stay can be but brief.
4.1.44–45

I pray you be acquainted with [me];
[I] come to do you good.
4.1.51–52

Will't please you walk aside?
4.1.59

I am your free dependent.
4.3.90

What, are you married?
5.1.172

Hold up your hands, say nothing: I'll speak all.
5.1.436

They say the best men are moulded out of faults,
And, for the most, become much more the better
For being a little bad.
5.1.437–39

THE MERRY WIVES OF WINDSOR

Would I were young for your sake!
1.1.238

[You two] shall be my East and West Indies, and I will
   trade to [you] both.

1.3.67–68

[I] speak but for [my] friend.

1.4.109

O, you are a flattering boy: now I see you'll be a courtier.

3.2.7–8

Have I caught thee, my heavenly jewel?

3.3.38

Thou wouldst make an absolute courtier.

3.3.55–56

The firm fixture of thy foot would give an excellent
   motion to thy gait in a semi-circled farthingale.

3.3.56–58

Od's heartlings, that's a pretty jest indeed!

3.4.56–57

A MIDSUMMER NIGHT'S DREAM

We [women] should be woo'd, and were not made
   to woo.

2.1.242

Where is my love?

5.1.252

O dainty duck! O dear!

5.1.270

Much Ado About Nothing

Well, I would you did like me.

2.1.92

I know you by the waggling of your head.

2.1.105

Will you not tell me who told you so? . . . Nor will you
   tell me who you are?

2.1.115,117

For which of my bad parts didst thou first fall in love
   with me?

5.2.56–57

But for which of my good parts did you first suffer love
   for me?

5.2.60–61

Thou and I are too wise to woo peaceably.

5.2.67

Othello

In following [you] I follow but myself.

1.1.57

I must show out a flag and sign of love.

1.1.153

      [Are] there not charms
By which the property of youth and maidhood
May be abused? Have you not read . . .
Of some such thing?

1.1.169–72

I think this tale would win my daughter too.

1.3.172

To my unfolding lend your prosperous ear
And let me find a charter in your voice
T'assist my simpleness.

1.3.245–46

What sayst thou, noble heart?

1.3.303

[You are a] great captain's captain.

2.1.74

What wouldst thou write of me, if thou shouldst
   praise me?

2.1.117

I am not merry, but I do beguile
The thing I am by seeming otherwise.
Come, how wouldst thou praise me?

2.1.122–24

[You can] think, and ne'er disclose [your] mind,
See suitors following, and not look behind.

2.1.156–57

It gives me wonder great as my content
To see you here before me.

2.1.181–82

Come hither: if thou be'st valiant—as, they say, base
   men being in love have then a nobility in their
   natures, more than is native to them.

2.1.212–15

Look if my gentle love be not raised up!

2.3.246

I think you think I love you.

2.3.306

[You're] framed as fruitful
As the free elements.

2.3.336–37

An unauthorized kiss!

4.1.2

Alas, poor rogue, I think i'faith [you] love me.

4.1.112

I may chance to see you, for I would very fain speak with
you.

4.1.163–64

Why, now I see there's mettle in thee, and even from
this instant do build on thee a better opinion than
ever before.

4.2.206–8

So sweet was ne'er so fatal.

5.2.20

PERICLES

With [you I've] liking took.

1.Chorus.25

Fair glass of light, I lov'd you, and could still.

1.1.77

It [is] certain you were not so bad.

1.1.126

I do not doubt thy faith.

1.2.111

Now, by the gods, [you] could not please me better.

2.3.72

Come, sir, here's a lady that wants breathing too;
And I have heard, you . . .
Are excellent in making ladies trip,
And that their measures are as excellent.

2.3.100–103

Then you love us, we you, and we'll clasp hands.

2.4.57

      I am beholding to you
For your sweet music this last night.

2.5.25–26

Come, other sorts offend as well as we.

4.2.34

I was mortally brought forth, and am
No other than I appear.

5.1.104–5

[You are] another Juno;
Who starves the ears she feeds, and makes them hungry
The more she gives them speech.

5.1.111–12

How achiev'd you these endowments which
You make more rich to owe?

5.1.116–17

If I should tell my history, 'twould seem
Like lies, disdain'd in the reporting.

5.1.118–19

I will believe thee,
And make my senses credit thy relation
To points that seem impossible.

5.1.122–24

Tell thy story;
If thine consider'd prove the thousandth part
Of my endurance, thou art a man, and I
Have suffer'd like a girl.

5.1.134–37

[You are] the rarest dream that e'er dulled sleep
Did mock sad fools withal.

5.1.161–62

ROMEO AND JULIET

What sadness lengthens [your] hours?

1.1.161

Good heart, at what [do you weep]?

1.1.182

Now my lord, what say you to my suit?

1.2.6

Woo [me] gentle . . . get [my] heart.

1.2.16

You have dancing shoes with nimble soles.

1.3.14–15

You are looked for and called for, asked for and sought
　　for.

1.5.12–13

Ah my mistresses, which of you all
Will now deny to dance?

1.5.18–19

It seems [you] doth hang upon the cheek of night
As a rich jewel in an Ethiop's ear.

1.5.44–45

Did my heart love till now? Forswear it, sight.
For I ne'er saw true beauty till this night.

1.5.51–52

Come hither, cover'd with an antic face.

1.5.55

[I am] bewitched by the charm of looks.

2.Prologue.6

[I'll] steal love's sweet bait from fearful hooks.

2.Prologue.8

Can I go forward when my heart is here?

2.1.1

[Your] eye discourses, I will answer it.

2.2.13

O speak again bright angel.

2.2.26

Thou art thyself.

2.2.39

I know not how to tell thee who I am.

2.2.54

My ears have yet not drunk a hundred words
Of thy tongue's uttering, yet I know the sound.

2.2.58–59

How cam'st thou hither, tell me, and wherefore?

2.2.62

Thou know'st the mask of night is on my face,
Else would a maiden blush bepaint my cheek
For that which thou hast heard me speak tonight.
Fain would I dwell on form; fain, fain deny
What I have spoke. But farewell, compliment.

2.2.85–89

Sweet, good night,
This bud of love, by summer's ripening breath,
May prove a beauteous flower when next we meet.

2.2.120–22

Good night, good night. As sweet repose and rest
Come to thy heart as that within my breast.

2.2.123–24

Three words . . . and good night indeed.

2.2.142

A thousand times good night.

2.2.154

I shall forget [why I did call thee], to have thee still stand
    there,
Remembering how I love thy company.

2.2.172–73

[In your presence I'm] forgetting any other home but
   this.

2.2.175

Good night, good night. Parting is such sweet sorrow
That I shall say good night till it be morrow.

2.2.184–85

Sleep dwell upon thine eyes, peace in thy breast.
Would I were sleep and peace so sweet to rest.

2.2.186–87

Virtue itself turns vice being misapplied,
And vice sometime's by action dignified.

2.3.17–18

What early tongue so sweet saluteth me?

2.3.28

O [you are] the courageous captain of compliments.

2.4.19–20

I desire some confidence with you.

2.4.126

      O so light a foot
Will ne'er wear out the everlasting flint.

2.6.16–17

Thy beauty hath made me effeminate.

3.1.116

A pack of blessings light upon thy back;
Happiness courts thee in her best array.

3.3.140–41

I have an interest in your hearts' proceeding.

3.1.190

I have more care to stay than will to go.

3.5.23

O think'st thou we shall ever meet again?

3.5.51

O, [you're] a lovely gentleman.

3.5.218

Thy face is mine.

4.1.35

How now, my headstrong: where have you been
     gadding?

4.2.16

[I am] a friend, and one that knows you well.

5.3.123

THE TAMING OF THE SHREW

     Is it possible
That love should of a sudden take such hold?

1.1.146–47

I love [you] ten times more than e'er I did.
O, how I long to have some chat with [you].

2.1.161–62

Entreat me how you can.

3.2.201

THE TEMPEST

Would I might but ever see [this] man!

1.2.168–69

There's nothing ill can dwell in such a temple:
If the ill spirit have so fair a house,
Good things will strive to dwell with 't.

1.2.460–62

The air breathes upon us here most sweetly.

2.1.45

Here comes a spirit.

2.2.15

Nor have I seen
More that I may call men than you, good friend.

3.1.50–51

Thou mak'st me merry; I am full of pleasure:
Let us be jocund.

3.2.114–15

Do you love me, master? no?

4.1.48

Let me live here ever.

4.1.122

I thank thee for that jest.

4.1.241

    Thou
Shalt have the air at freedom; for a little
Follow, and do me service.

4.1.264–66

Whether thou be'st . . .
Some enchanted trifle to abuse me,
. . . I not know: thy pulse
Beats, as of flesh and blood.

5.1.111–14

How beauteous mankind is!

5.1.183

My tricksy spirit!

5.1.226

    I long
To hear the story of your life, which must
Take the ear strangely.

5.1.311–13

Let me not . . . dwell
In this bare island by your spell;
But release me from my band
With help of your good hands.

Epilogue.5–10

TROILUS AND CRESSIDA

If [you] be fair, 'tis the better for [you]; and [you] be
   not, [you] have the mends in [your] own hands.

1.1.67–68

[This] is too flaming a praise for a good complexion.

1.2.105–6

[You're] a merry Greek indeed.

1.2.110

How [you] look, and how [you] go!

1.2.237

You are such a woman, a man knows not at what ward
you lie.

1.2.263–64

Yet hold I off. Women are angels, wooing:
Things won are done; joy's soul lies in the doing.

1.2.291–92

She belov'd knows naught that knows not this:
Men prize the thing ungain'd more than it is.

1.2.293–94

She was never yet that ever knew
Love got so sweet as when desire did sue.

1.2.295–96

You speak
Like one besotted on your sweet delights.

2.2.143–44

You are full of fair words.

3.1.46

[You] do so blush, and fetch [your] wind so short, as if
[you] were frayed with a spirit!

3.2.29–31

They say all lovers swear more performance than they
are able, and yet reserve an ability that they never
perform: vowing more than the perfection of ten and
discharging less than the tenth par of one.

3.2.83–87

Where is my wit? I know not what I speak.
                              3.2.149

Dear, trouble not yourself; the morn is cold.
                              4.2.1

You smile and mock me, as if I meant naughtily.
                              4.2.38

Lady, give me your hand, and, as we walk,
To our own selves bend we our needful talk.
                              4.4.136–37

TWELFTH NIGHT

Wit, and't be thy will, put me into good fooling!
                              1.5.30

Here comes the trout that must be caught with tickling.
                              2.5.21–22

Love knows I love;
But who?
Lips, do not move,
No man must know.
                              2.5.98–101

I warrant thou art a merry fellow, and car'st for nothing.
                              3.1.26–27

Why then methinks 'tis time to smile again.
O world, how apt the poor are to be proud!
If one should be a prey, how much the better
To fall before the lion than the wolf!
                              3.1.128–31

Be not afraid, good youth, I will not have you,
And yet when wit and youth is come to harvest,
Your wife is like to reap a proper man.

3.1.133–35

I prithee tell me what thou think'st of me.

3.1.140

Assure thyself there is no love-broker in the world can
   more prevail in man's commendation with woman
   than report of valour.

3.2.35–37

Lead me on.

3.4.381

Give me thy hand.

5.1.270

THE TWO GENTLEMEN OF VERONA

Were 't not affection chains thy tender days
To the sweet glances of thy honour'd love,
I rather would entreat thy company
To see the wonders of the world abroad.

1.1.3–6

Wish me partaker in thy happiness,
When thou dost meet good hap.

1.1.14–15

[Pray for me] on some shallow story of deep love.

1.1.21

That's a deep story of a deeper love,
For [I am] more than over shoes in love.

1.1.23–24

Let me hear from thee by letters.

1.1.57

Wouldst thou then counsel me to fall in love?

1.2.2

Maids, in modesty, say 'no' to that
Which they would have the profferer construe 'ay'.

1.2.55–56

Some love of yours hath writ to you in rhyme.

1.2.79

I shun the fire, for fear of burning.

1.3.78

      Give it me, it's mine.
Sweet ornament, that decks a thing divine!

2.1.4–5

Why, how know you that I am in love?

2.1.16

[You know you are in love] by these special marks: first
you have learned . . . to wreathe your arms like a
malcontent; to relish a love-song, like a robin-
redbreast; to walk alone, like one that had the
pestilence; to sigh, like a schoolboy that had lost his
ABC; to weep, like a young wench that had buried
her grandam; to fast, like one that takes diet; to
watch, like one that fears robbing; to speak puling,
like a beggar at Hallowmas.

2.1.17–25

Why, lady, Love hath twenty pair of eyes.

2.4.71–72

My tales of love were wont to weary you:
I know you joy not in a love-discourse.

2.4.121–22

Love, lend me wings to make my purpose swift
As thou hast lent me wit to plot this drift.

2.6.42–43

A woman sometimes scorns what best contents her.

3.1.93

Scorn at first makes after-love the more.

3.1.96–97

Why, this it is to be a peevish girl,
That flies her fortune when it follows her.

5.2.48–49

THE WINTER'S TALE

We two will walk.

1.2.172

    I am angling now,
Though you perceive me not how I give line.

1.2.180–81

Come, quench your blushes, and present yourself
That which you are.

4.4.67–68

Your praises are too large.

4.4.147

I'll blush you thanks.

4.4.585

When she has obtain'd your eye,
Will have your tongue too.

5.1.105–6

Enticements and Inducements

GIVING GIFTS is not really giving. It's seduction. It's extra incentive. It's temptation laced with expectation, creating obligation and hopefully leading to reciprocation. No present is ever free of strings, and Shakespeare knew it.

Promises, enticements, oaths, tokens, and all these engines of lust . . . many a maid hath been seduced by them.

Yet many enticements aren't enticing enough. Common wisdom says the best offer wins the prize. But when competition is keen, it's the way you offer—not the best offer—that makes you uncommon. Make yourself exceptional with Shakespeare's sensational expressions. If you're rich, say you'll set that certain someone in a shower of gold and hail pearls upon them. If you're not: say you'd love to fleet the time together carelessly as they did in the golden world. Anything you offer will glitter and glister when you wrap it in Shakespeare.

Real giving is from the heart and mind, and the stuff of the mind is language. Shakespeare makes it shimmer, so make his way with words yours. The following pages offer more to come. It's the power of promise that matters.

In fact, stop with the promises. Save yourself the gifts. Shakespeare's phrases are so rich that anything you give just pales in comparison. The paper is worth more than the present. Don't disappoint the one who delights you. Promise fairies to attend and fetch jewels from the deep. Or couch your souls on flowers and make the ghosts gaze. Be generous with words. What other gift could possibly compare to the imagination of a first-rate genius?

Antony and Cleopatra

There's not a minute of our lives should stretch
Without some pleasure now. What sport tonight?

1.1.47–48

Mine, and most of our fortunes tonight, shall be drunk
  to bed.

1.2.47–48

Let witchcraft join with beauty, lust with both;
Tie up the libertine in a field of feasts;
Keep his brain fuming.

2.1.22–24

          Here
My bluest veins to kiss, a hand that kings
Have lipped, and trembled, a kissing.

2.5.30

I'll set thee in a shower of gold and hail
Rich pearls upon thee.

2.5.45–46

          [I] partly beg
To be desired to give. It much would please [me]
That of [my] fortunes you should make a staff
To lean upon.

3.13.70–73

Where souls do couch on flowers we'll hand in hand
And with our sprightly port make the ghosts gaze.

4.14.52–53

As You Like It

[Let us] fleet the time carelessly as they did in the golden
  world.

  1.1.118–19

When I break that oath, let me turn monster.

  1.2.20–21

[I] wish, for [your] sake more than for mine own,
My fortunes were more able to relieve [you].

  2.4.74–75

Come, woo me, woo me; for now I am in a holiday
  humour and like enough to consent.

  4.1.65–66

Come, now I will be your [lover] in a more coming-on
  disposition; and ask me what you will, I will grant it.

  4.1.106–8

[I'll have you to wife] as fast as she can marry us.

  4.1.127

Believe . . . if you please, that I can do strange things.

  5.2.58–60

If you will be married tomorrow, you shall.

  5.2.72–73

Cymbeline

I dedicate myself to your sweet pleasure.

  1.7.136

I am advised to give [you] music a mornings, they say it
  will penetrate.

2.3.11–12

HAMLET

If there be any good thing to be done
That may to thee do ease and grace to me,
Speak to me.

1.1.133–35

[I am] colleagued with this dream of [your] advantage.

1.2.21

What wouldst thou beg,
That shall not be my offer, not thy asking?

1.2.45–46

What wouldst thou have.

1.2.50

Let ply music.

2.1.72

Your visitation shall receive such thanks
As fits a king's remembrance.

2.2.25–26

Go to your rest, at night we'll feast together.

2.2.84

And for my means, I'll husband them so well,
They shall go far with little.

4.5.138–39

Repair thou to me with as much speed as thou wouldest fly
   death.

4.6.21–22

You must put me in your heart for friend.

4.7.2

Love's Labour's Lost

I will tell thee wonders.

1.2.130

We number nothing that we spend for you:
Our duty is so rich, so infinite,
That we may do it still without account.

5.2.198–200

        Mistress, look on me,
Behold the window of my heart, mine eye,
What humble suit attends thy answer there;
Impose some service on me for thy love.

5.2.829–32

Measure for Measure

Always obedient to your Grace's will,
I come to know your pleasure.

1.1.25–26

I'll bribe you . . . with such gifts that heaven shall share
   with you.

2.2.146–48

I have provided for you; stay a while.

2.3.17

I am come to know your pleasure.

2.4.31

Thou a feverous life shouldst entertain.

3.1.74

I have spirit to do anything that appears not foul in the
truth of my spirit.

3.1.205–6

What pleasure [are you] given to?

3.2.228

May be I will call upon you anon for some advantage to
yourself.

4.1.22–24

Take . . . this your companion by the hand,
Who hath a story ready for your ear.

4.1.55–56

    [I] desire [you]
To try [your] gracious fortune with [me].

5.1.78–79

        All my life to come
I'll lend you all my life to do you service.

5.1.429–30

I have a motion much imports your good;
Whereto if you'll a willing ear incline,
What's mine is yours, and what is yours is mine.

5.1.532–34

THE MERRY WIVES OF WINDSOR

It were a goot motion if we leave our pribbles and
   prabbles, and desire a marriage.

1.1.51–52

[I] shall tell you another tale, if matters grow to your
   likings.

1.1.70–71

We have appointed to dine . . . and I would not break
   with [you] for more money than I'll speak of.

3.2.49–51

A MIDSUMMER NIGHT'S DREAM

        [I have] given [you] rhymes,
And interchang'd love-tokens with [you]:
[I have] by moonlight at [your] window sung
With faining voice verses of feigning love,
And stol'n the impression of [your] fantasy
With bracelets of [my] hair, rings, gauds, conceits,
Knacks, rifles, nosegays, sweetmeats (messengers
Of strong prevailment in unharden'd youth):

1.1.28–35

Run through fire I will for thy sweet sake!

2.2.102

I'll give thee fairies to attend on thee;
And they shall fetch thee jewels from the deep,
And sing, while thou on pressed flowers dost sleep.

3.1.150–52

Now thou and I are new in amity,
And will to-morrow midnight, solemnly,
Dance in Duke Theseus' house triumphantly.
                              4.1.86–88

We will, fair queen, up to the mountain's top,
And mark the musical confusion
Of hounds and echo in conjunction.
                              4.1.108–10

Come now; what masques, what dances shall we have!
                              5.1.32

What revels are in hand?
                              5.1.36

What masque, what music? How shall we beguile
The lazy time, if not with some delight?
                              5.1.40–41

MUCH ADO ABOUT NOTHING

[I will write you] a sonnet in praise of [your] beauty in
    so high a style . . . that no man living shall come over
    it, for in most comely truth thou deservest it.
                              5.2.4–8

OTHELLO

I will a round unvarnished tale deliver
Of my whole course of love, what drugs, what charms,
What conjuration and what mighty magic.
                              1.3.91–93

Our loves and comforts should increase
Even as our days do grow.
                                                    2.1.192–93

Honey, you shall be well desired.
                                                    2.1.203

[I have] devoted and given up [my]self to the
      contemplation, mark and denotement of [your] parts
      and graces.
                                                    2.3.311–13

I will bestow you where you shall have time
To speak your bosom freely.
                                                    3.1.56–57

I [am] nothing, but to please [your] fantasy.
                                                    3.3.303

Do not you chide, I have a thing for you.
                                                    3.3.305

If you'll come to supper tonight, you may; if you will not,
      come when you are next prepared for.
                                                    4.1.157–58

What is your pleasure?
                                                    4.2.24

Come, stand not amazed . . . but go along with me.
                                                    4.2.240–41

PERICLES

[I'll] sing a song that old was sung . . .
To glad your ear, and please your eyes.
1.Chorus.1–4

Day serves not light more faithful than I'll be.
1.2.110

Were my fortunes equal to my desires, I could wish to
  make one [with you].
2.1.110–11

Prepare for mirth.
2.3.7

Come, queen o' th' feast!
2.3.17

[I have] bent all offices to honour [you].
2.5.48

  My recompense is thanks, that's all;
Yet my good will is great, though the gift small.
3.4.16–17

Do not consume your blood with sorrowing:
Have you a nurse of me!
4.1.23–24

Instruct [me] what [I have] to do, that [I] may not be
  raw in [my] entertainment.
4.2.50–52

He that will give most shall have [me] first.
4.2.55–56

You shall live in pleasure.

4.2.72

ROMEO AND JULIET

How stands your dispositions to be married?

1.3.65

So shall you share all that [I] do possess,
By having [me], making yourself no less.

1.3.93–94

All my fortunes at thy foot I'll lay,
And follow thee . . . throughout the world.

2.2.147–48

O for a falconer's voice
To lure this tassel-gentle back again.

2.2.158–59

[I] toil in your delight.

2.5.76

[I] shall happily make thee . . . a joyful bride.

3.5.115

[I'll give you] what becomed love I might,
Not stepping o'er the bounds of modesty.

4.2.26–27

THE TEMPEST

This music crept by me upon the waters,
Allaying both their fury and my passion
With its sweet air.

1.2.394–96

If a virgin,
And your affection not gone forth, I'll make you
The Queen of Naples.

1.2.450–52

Thou shalt be as free as mountain winds.

1.2.501–2

Beseech you, sir, be merry.

2.1.1

[I] will become thy bed, I warrant,
And bring thee forth brave brood.

3.2.102–3

Thy thoughts I cleave to. What's thy pleasure?

4.1.164

TWELFTH NIGHT

If music be the food of love, play on,
Give me excess of it, that, surfeiting,
The appetite may sicken, and so die.

1.1.1–3

O, [music] came o'er my ear like the sweet sound
That breathes upon a bank of violets,
Stealing and giving odour.

1.1.5–7

So full of shapes is fancy,
That it alone is high fantastical.

1.1.14–15

Away before me to sweet beds of flowers!
Love-thoughts lie rich when canopied with bowers.

1.1.40–41

What I am, and what I would, are as secret as
    maidenhead: to your ears, divinity; to any other's,
    profanation.

1.5.218–20

Here, wear this jewel for me, 'tis my picture:
Refuse it not, it hath no tongue to vex you:
And I beseech you come again to-morrow.

3.4.210–12

If thou entertain'st my love, let it appear in thy smiling, thy
    smiles become thee well. Therefore in my presence still
    smile, dear my sweet, I prithee.

2.5.175–77

THE TWO GENTLEMEN OF VERONA

Here is my hand, for my true constancy.

2.2.8

A thousand oaths, an ocean of [my] tears,
And instances of infinite of love,
Warrant [you] welcome.

2.7.69–71

[I'll] win [you] with gifts, if [you] respect not words:
Dumb jewels often in their silent kind,
More than quick words, do move a woman's mind.

3.1.89–91

Upon the altar of [your] beauty
[I] sacrifice [my] tears, [my] sighs, [my] heart.

3.2.72–73

[I] write till [my] ink be dry; and with [my] tears
Moist it again; and frame some feeling line
That may discover such integrity.

3.2.74–76

Madam, this service I have done for you
(Though you respect not aught your servant doth)
To hazard life, and rescue you from him
That would have forc'd your honour and your love.

5.4.19–22

What dangerous action, stood it next to death,
Would I not undergo, for one calm look?

5.4.41–42

The Winter's Tale

This entertainment
May a free face put on, derive a liberty
From heartiness, from bounty, fertile bosom,
And well become the agent: 't may, I grant:

1.2.111–14

[I am] most goddess-like prank'd up.

4.4.10

Apprehend
Nothing but jollity.

4.4.24–25

See, your guests approach:
Address yourself to entertain them sprightly,
And let's be red with mirth.

4.4.52–54

My fair'st friend,
I would I had some flowers o' th' spring, that might
Become your time of day.

4.4.112–14

Come! come buy! come buy!
Buy, lads, or else your lasses cry.

4.4.230–31

I know
[You] prize not such trifles as these are:
The gifts [you] look from me are pack'd and lock'd
Up in my heart, which I have given already,
But not deliver'd.

4.4.357–61

Self-Inflation

PEOPLE HAVE A WEAKNESS for power. And you can acquire an aura of power the way lots of Shakespeare's figures do: by being big. Shakespeare knows that a person has to be enormous to impress anyone in this jaded world.

Othello is huge in Desdemona's maiden mind from stories of sieges and treasure. Petruchio wears chaos like an oversized overcoat. Falstaff is a great distended bladder of bravismo. Just as Shakespeare's language enlarges them, it can pump you up in the eyes of the one you desire. You, too, can balloon with vitality. His words make you bigger than you are.

Don't think this is dishonesty. Everywhere in the animal world you see this magic at work in the mating display. Little creatures puff up into big ones. It's natural PR. Think peacocks and puffer fish. Just follow your instincts, inflatable species that you are. That swollen head, even fatter than usual, can be hugely attractive as long as it's stuffed with Shakespeare.

Human beings have to compensate for being furless and featherless. Be true to your biology. Get your quarry to believe passionately that your passions are made of nothing but the finest part of true love. Inventory your honorable parts for them. Advertise what a pretty piece of flesh you are. If you lack real stature, imply potential. If you have nothing at all, you still have words and the breath to breathe them. Inhale deeply and expand your prospects. Imagination is the human version of colorful tail feathers. Display the verbiage with the finest plumage. Shake your Shakespeare.

ALL'S WELL THAT ENDS WELL

[Here] shall [you] have a thousand loves,
A mother, and a mistress, and a friend,
A phoenix, captain, and an enemy,
A guide, a goddess, and a sovereign,
A counsellor, a traitress, and a dear.

1.1.162–66

My friends were poor, but honest; so's my love.

1.3.190

     This youthful parcel
Of noble bachelors stand at my bestowing.

2.3.52–53

I am a simple maid, and therein wealthiest
That I protest I simply am a maid.

2.3.66–67

And my integrity ne'er knew the crafts
That you do charge men with.

4.2.33–34

ANTONY AND CLEOPATRA

[My] passions are made of nothing but the finest part of
    pure love.

1.2.153–54

Though age from folly could not give me freedom,
It does from childishness.

1.3.58–59

The world and my great office will sometimes
Divide me from your bosom.

2.3.1–2

           Though grey
Do something mingle with [my] younger brown, yet
      have [I]
A brain that nourishes [my] nerves and can
Get goal for goal of youth.

4.8.19–22

As You Like It

Though I look old, yet I am strong and lusty.

2.3.47

My age is as a lusty winter.

2.3.52

I'll do the service of a younger man
In all your business and necessities.

2.3.53–55

I will follow thee to the last gasp with truth and loyalty.

2.3.69–70

I must comfort the weaker vessel, as doublet and hose
    ought to show itself courageous to petticoat; therefore
    courage.

2.4.4–7

'Tis not [my] glass but you that flatters [me],
And out of you [I] see [my]self more proper
Than any of [my] lineaments can show [me].

3.5.54–56

Mistress, know yourself. Down on your knees
And thank heaven, fasting, for a good man's love.
                                                    3.5.57–58

I have neither the scholar's melancholy, which is
    emulation; nor the musician's, which is fantastical;
    nor the courtier's, which is proud; nor the soldier's,
    which is ambitious; nor the lawyer's, which is politic;
    nor the lady's, which is nice; nor the lover's, which is
    all these; but it is a melancholy of mine own,
    compounded of many simples, extracted from many
    objects, and indeed the sundry contemplation of my
    travels.
                                                    4.1.10–18

I will be more jealous of thee than a Barbary cock-pigeon
    over his hen, more clamorous than a parrot against
    rain, more new-fangled than an ape, more giddy in my
    desires than a monkey.
                                                    4.1.141–45

[If] thou didst know how many fathom deep I am in
    love!
                                                    4.1.195–96

[The depth of my love] cannot be sounded.
                                                    4.1.197

I have trod a measure, I have flattered a lady, I have been
    politic with my friend, smooth with mine enemy, I
    have undone three tailors, I have had four quarrels,
    and like to have fought one.
                                                    5.4.44–47

I am not furnished like a beggar, therefore to beg will not
    become me. My way is to conjure you.
                                                    5.4.206–8

CYMBELINE

I will remain the loyal'st husband that e'er did plight
   troth.

1.2.26–27

   Breathe [my] faults so quaintly
That they may seem the taints of liberty,
The flash and outbreak of a fiery mind,
A savageness in unreclaimed blood.

2.1.31–34

HAMLET

[I am] a man faithful and honourable.

2.2.130

[I] send some precious instance of [my]self
After the thing [I] love.

4.5.162–63

Eat a crocodile? I'll do't.

5.1.271–72

[I am] an absolute gentleman, full of most excellent
   differences, of very soft society and great showing.

5.2.107–8

[I am] the card or calendar of gentry; for you shall find
   in [me] the continent of what part a gentleman
   would see.

5.2.109–11

I am satisfied in nature.

5.2.240

Love's Labour's Lost

[I] have measur'd many miles
To tread a measure with [you] on this grass.

5.2.184–85

Measure for Measure

I love the people
But do not like to stage me to their eyes.

1.1.67–68

[My] purpose [is]
More grave and wrinkled than the aims and ends
Of burning youth.

1.3.4–6

As those that feed grow full, as blossoming time
That from the seedness the bare fallow brings
To teeming foison, even so [my] plenteous womb
Expresseth [your] full tilth and husbandry.

1.4.41–44

I think and pray
To several subjects: Heaven hath my empty words,
Whilst my invention, hearing not my tongue,
Anchors on [you].

2.4.1–4

I have no superfluous leisure; my stay must be stolen out
of other affairs: but I will attend you a while.

3.1.156–58

Fasten your ear on my advisings, to the love I have in
doing good.

3.1.196–97

[I have] some feeling of the sport; [I know] the service;
and that instruct[s] [me] to mercy.

3.2.115–17

Mark what I say, which you shall find
By every syllable a faithful verity.

4.3.125–26

You shall see how I'll handle [you].

5.1.270–71

You may marvel why I obscur'd myself.

5.1.388

The Merry Wives of Windsor

[I] have brown hair, and speak small like a woman.

1.1.44–45

Setting the attraction of my good parts aside, I have no
other charms.

2.2.100–1

Ay, be-gar, and de maid is love-a me.

3.2.58

[I] caper, [I] dance, [I have] eyes of youth; [I] write
verses, [I] speak holiday, [I] smell April and May.

3.2.60–62

A Midsummer Night's Dream

I am . . . as well deriv'd as he,
As well possess'd; my love is more than his;

My fortunes every way as fairly rank'd,
If not with vantage, as [his].

1.1.99–102

I am that merry wanderer of the night.

2.1.43

And then end life when I end loyalty!

2.2.62

I am a spirit of no common rate;
The summer still doth tend upon my state;
And I do love thee: therefore go with me.

3.1.147–49

MUCH ADO ABOUT NOTHING

But it is certain I am loved of all ladies, only you
excepted.

1.1.114–15

OTHELLO

By the faith of man I know my price, I am worth no
worse.

1.1.9–10

In simple and pure soul I come to you.

1.1.106

> Do not believe
> That from the sense of all civility
> I thus would play and trifle with [you].

1.1.130

[I am] a maiden never bold,
Of spirit so still and quiet that [my] motion
Blushed at [my]self.

1.3.95–97

Question me the story of my life
From year to year—the battles, sieges, fortunes
That I have passed.
I [will] it through, even from my boyish days
To th' very moment that [you bid] me tell it.

1.3.130–34

[I'll speak] of most disastrous chances,
Of moving accidents by flood and field,
Of hair-breadth scapes i'th' imminent deadly breach,
Of being taken by the insolent foe
And sold to slavery; of my redemption thence
And portance in my travailous history;
Wherein of antres vast and deserts idle,
Rough quarries, rocks and hills whose heads touch
    heaven
[Give me] my hint to speak.

1.3.139–43

Upon [your] hint I spake:
[You] loved me for the dangers I had passed
And I loved [you] that [you] did pity them.
This is the only witchcraft I have used.

1.3.167–70

Let it not gall your patience . . .
That I extend my manners; 'tis my breeding
That gives me this bold show of courtesy.

2.1.97–99

[I am] so free, so kind, so apt, so blest a disposition that
    [I] hold it a vice in [my] goodness not to do more
    than [I am] requested.

                                        2.3.315–17

It were not for your quiet nor your good
Nor for my manhood, honesty and wisdom
To let you know my thoughts.

                                        3.3.155–57

[You] had eyes and chose me.

                                        3.3.192

You may indeed say [my hand is good],
For 'twas that hand that gave away my heart.

                                        3.4.44–45

PERICLES

[I'm] so great can make [my] will [my] act.

                                        1.2.19

He loves you well that holds his life of you.

                                        2.2.22

My actions are as noble as my thoughts.

                                        2.5. 58

O, you have heard something of my power, and so stand
    aloof for more serious wooing.

                                        4.6.85–87

I protest to thee, pretty one, my authority shall . . . look
    friendly upon thee.

                                        4.6.87–89

[Gaze on me]. Is't not a goodly presence?

5.1.65

I am a maid,
. . . that ne'er before invited eyes,
But have been gaz'd on like a comet.

5.1.84–86

ROMEO AND JULIET

'Tis known I am a pretty piece of flesh.

1.1.28

I'll go along, [new love] to be shown,
But to rejoice in splendour of mine own.

1.2.102–3

Nay I do bear a brain.

1.3.29

I have seen the day
That I have worn a visor and could tell
A whispering tale in a fair lady's ear,
Such as would please.

1.5.21–24

I conjure thee by [my] bright eyes,
By [my] high forehead and [my] scarlet lip,
By [my] fine foot, straight leg, and quivering thigh,
And the demesnes that there adjacent lie,
That in thy likeness thou appear to [me].

2.1.17–21

With love's light wings did I o'er perch these walls,
For stony limits cannot hold love out,
And what love can do, that dares love attempt.

2.2.66–68

I am the very pink of courtesy.

2.4.59

I saw no man use you at his pleasure; if I had, my
    weapon should quickly have been out.

2.4.154–55

[I am] a gentleman of noble parentage,
Of fair demesnes, youthful and nobly lign'd.

3.5.179–80

[I am] stuff'd as they say, with honourable parts.

3.5.181

[I am] proportion'd as one's thought would wish a man.

3.5.182

An eagle, madam,

Hath not so green, so quick, so fair an eye
As [I have].

3.5.219–21

THE TAMING OF THE SHREW

Thou must be married to no man but me.
For I am he am born to tame you, Kate,
And bring you from a wild Kate to a Kate
Conformable as other household Kates.

2.1.268–71

I tell you 'tis incredible to believe
How much [women] love me.

2.1.299–300

I read that I profess, The Art to Love.

4.2.8

THE TEMPEST

My zenith doth depend upon
A most auspicious star, whose influence
If now I court not, but omit, my fortunes
Will ever after droop.

1.2.181–84

I flam'd amazement.

1.2.198

My spirits are nimble.

2.1.197

Look how well my garments sit upon me.

2.1.267

My sweet mistress
Weeps when she sees me work, and says, such baseness
Had never like executor.

3.1.11–13

I had rather crack my sinews, break my back,
Than you should such dishonour undergo,
While I sit lazy by.

3.1.26–28

As I hope
For quiet days, fair issue and long life,
With such love as 'tis now, the murkiest den,
The most opportune place, the strong'st suggestion
Our worser genius can, shall never melt
Mine honour into lust.

4.1.23–28

TROILUS AND CRESSIDA

Have you any eyes? Do you know what a man is? Is not
birth, beauty, good shape, discourse, manhood,
learning, gentleness, virtue, youth, liverality and such
like, the spice and salt that season a man?

1.2.256–60

{I} vow to weep seas, live in fire, eat rocks, tame tigers;
thinking it harder for {my} mistress to devise
imposition enough than for {me} to undergo any
difficulty imposed.

3.2.75–79

Though {I} be long ere {I} be wooed, {I am} constant
being won.

3.2.109–10

I am as true as truth's simplicity,
And simpler than the infancy of truth.

3.2.167–68

I can sing,
And speak to [you] in many sorts of music.

1.2.57–58

[I] play o' th' viol-de-gamboys, and speak three or four
    languages word for word without book, and hath all
    the good gifts of nature.

1.3.25–28

Look you, sir, such a one I was this present. Is't not well
    done?

1.5.237–38

O sir, I will not be so hard-hearted: I will give out divers
    schedules of my beauty. I shall be inventoried, and
    every particle and utensil labelled to my will. As,
    item, two lips indifferent red; item, two grey eyes,
    with lids to them; item, one neck, one chin, and so
    forth. Were you sent hither to praise me?

1.5.247–53

Come hither, boy. If ever thou shalt love,
In the sweet pangs of it remember me:
For such as I am, all true lovers are,
Unstaid and skittish in all motions else,
Save in the constant image of the creature
That is belov'd. How dost thou like this tune?

2.4.15–20

Alas, [women's] love may be call'd appetite,
No motion of the liver, but the palate,
That suffers surfeit, cloyment, and revolt;
But mine is all as hungry as the sea,
And can digest as much. Make no compare

Between that love a woman can bear me
And that I owe [a woman].
2.4.98–104

THE TWO GENTLEMEN OF VERONA

O flatter me; for love delights in praises.
2.4.143

Have I not reason to prefer mine own?
2.4.151

If you knew [my] pure heart's truth,
You would quickly learn to know [me] by [my] voice.
4.2.85–86

Fear not: [I] bear an honourable mind,
And will not use a woman lawlessly.
5.3.12–13

THE WINTER'S TALE

Our praises are our wages.
1.2.94

[I'll] wear you like [a] medal, hanging
About [my] neck.
1.2.307–8

I'll give no blemish to [your] honour, none.
1.2.341

        The gods themselves,
Humbling their deities to love, have taken
The shapes of beasts upon them: Jupiter

Became a bull, and bellow'd; the green Neptune
A ram, and bleated; and the fire-rob'd god,
Golden Apollo, a poor humble swain,
As I seem now.

4.4.25-31

      My desires
Run not before mine honour, nor my lusts
Burn hotter than my faith.

4.4.33-35

[I have] the prettiest love-songs for maids, so without
    bawdry (which is strange); with such delicate
    burdens of dildoes and fadings, jump her and thump
    her; and where some stretch-mouthed rascal would,
    as it were, mean mischief and break a foul gap into
    the matter, he makes the maid to answer 'Whoop, do
    me no harm, good man.'

4.4.194-201

Ego-Stroking

YOU CAN INFLATE YOURSELF only so much in front of someone before you need to pump them up, too. Their opinion of self must be big enough for them to think they're big enough for you. It's the bliss of size gazing into the eyes of size, a lovers' moon in the flesh, the soft glow of their fullness reflecting loveliness on you.

Shakespeare knew well how flattery lubricates the human condition. It makes the world as we know it move easily with the world as it actually is. Shakespeare's plays are filled with characters getting their psyches oiled. Cleopatra semi-deifies Antony, calling him the demi-Atlas of this earth. A brace of wives admires the greatness of Falstaff, to lead him where they merrily will. Olivia fawns over Viola, oblivious to the obvious. When the twin brother suddenly shows up, even futile flattery works! The stroking of your quarry's ego is potentially explosive, unleashing pent-up passion for self. The pages that follow are flashpaper.

The risk of burnt fingers is worth it. If people aren't praised, confidence in the human race collapses, taking down much that is admirable. People want it, people need it, so do it. Far from being selfish, your devotion to seduction makes the world more human. This truth is so disgusting it's wonderful: You participate in true reality only by indulging in flattery.

Shakespeare knows the nose and how to lead somebody by it. He knows how to sniff out your desired's sadly neglected qualities. At the first whiff of what's probably never been complimented, make your move. Try saying something as small as "How prettily you wash." But beware: if you inflate someone, you might believe your own words and seduce yourself.

All's Well That Ends Well

You were born under a charitable star.

1.1.186

Frank nature, rather curious than in haste,
Hath well compos'd thee.

1.2.20–21

Thus, Indian-like,
Religious in mine error, I adore
The sun that looks upon his worshipper
But knows of him no more.

1.3.199–202

Now by my faith and honour,
If seriously I may convey my thoughts
In this my light deliverance, I have spoke
With one that in her sex, her years, profession,
Wisdom and constancy, hath amaz'd me more
Then I dare blame my weakness.

2.1.79–84

Thy life is dear, for all that life can rate
Worth name of life in thee hath estimate:
Youth, beauty, wisdom, courage—all
That happiness and prime can happy call.

2.1.178–81

[This is] a showing of a heavenly effect in an earthly
    actor.

2.3.23

Honour, sir . . . flames in your fair eyes.

2.3.80–81

[You] are young, wise, fair;
In these to nature [you're] immediate heir,
And these breed honour.

2.3.131–33

Titled goddess;
And worth it, with addition!

4.2.2–3

[Your] beauty did astonish the survey
Of richest eyes.

5.3.16–17

[Your] words all ears took captive.

5.3.17

ANTONY AND CLEOPATRA

Fie, wrangling queen,
Whom everything becomes—to chide, to laugh,
To weep; whose every passion fully strives
To make itself, in thee, fair and admired!

1.1.49–52

You shall be yet far fairer than you are.

1.2.18

We cannot call [your] winds and waters sighs and tears;
they are greater storms and tempests than almanacs
can report.

1.2.154–56

[If I had never seen you, I] had then left unseen a
wonderful piece of work, which not to have been blest
withal would have discredited [my] travel.

1.2.160–62

[You] demi-Atlas of this earth, the arm
And burgonet of men!

1.5.24-25

[Your] beauty claims
No worse a husband than the best of men.

2.2.135-36

[Your] virtue and . . . general graces speak
That which none else can utter.

2.2.137-38

[You're] most triumphant lady, if report be
square to [you].

2.2.194-95

The air . . . for vacancy,
Had gone to gaze on [you]
And made a gap in nature.

2.2.226-28

Age cannot wither [you], nor custom stale [your]
    infinite variety.

2.2. 245-46

Other women cloy
The appetites they feed, but [you] make hungry
Where most [you] satisfy.

2.2.246-48

[You]

Should have an army for an usher, and
The neighs of horse to tell of her approach
Long ere [you] did appear. The trees by th' way
Should have borne men, and expectation fainted,
Longing for what it had not. Nay, the dust

Should have ascended to the roof of heaven,
Raised by your populous troops.

> 3.6.45–51

[You] wear the rose
Of youth upon [you].

> 3.13.20

O infinite virtue! Com'st thou smiling from
The world's great snare uncaught?

> 4.8.17–18

[Your] legs bestrid the ocean; [your] reared arm
Crested the world; [your] voice was propertied
As all the tuned spheres, and that to friends;
But when [you] meant to quail and shake the orb,
[You were] as rattling thunder.

> 5.2.81–85

For [your] bounty,
There was no winter in't; an autumn it was
That grew the more by reaping.

> 5.2.85–87

AS YOU LIKE IT

Report speaks goldenly of [your] profit.

> 1.1.5–6

They say many young gentlemen flock to [you] every
    day.

> 1.1.116–17

Yet [you're] gentle, never schooled and yet learned, full
  of noble device, of all sorts enchantingly beloved . . .
  so much in the heart of the world.

1.1.164–67

Thou speak'st wiser than thou art ware of.

2.4.54

O wonderful, wonderful! And most wonderful
  wonderful! And yet again wonderful! And after that
  out of all whooping.

3.2.188–90

[You are] true in love.

3.4.24

    The best thing in [you]
Is [your] complexion; and faster than [your] tongue
Did make offence, [your] eye did heal it up.

3.5.115–17

There was a pretty redness in [your] lip,
A little riper and more lusty red
Than that mix'd in [your] cheek; 'twas just the
  difference
Betwixt the constant red and mingled damask.

3.5.120–23

There be some women . . . had they mark'd [you]
In parcels as I did, would have gone near
To fall in love with [you].

3.5.124–26

[You] have a pretty wit.

5.1.28

I do remember in [you]
Some lively touches.

5.4.26–27

CYMBELINE

I do not think
So fair an outward, and such stuff within
Endows a man, but [you].

1.1.22–23

[You are]
A man worth any woman: overbuys me
Almost the sum [you] pay.

1.2.76–78

[You are] the gift of the gods.

1.5.82

All of [you] that is out of door most rich!
If [you] be furnish'd with a mind so rare,
[You are] alone th'Arabian bird.

1.7.15–17

[You are] one of the noblest note.

1.7.22

Heaven's bounty . . . in you [is] beyond all talents.

1.7.78–80

A lady
So fair, and fasten'd to an empery
Would make the great'st king double.

1.7.119–21

[You are] the best feather of our wing.

1.7.186

'Tis [your] breathing that
Perfumes the chamber thus.

2.2.18–19

Ah, but some natural notes about [your] body
Above ten thousand meaner moveables
Would testify, t'enrich mine inventory.

2.2.28–30

With every thing that pretty is, my lady sweet arise:
Arise, arise!

2.3.24–25

[You] did it with
A pudency so rosy, the sweet view on't
Might well have warm'd old Saturn.

2.4.162–64

O noble stain!
O worthiness of nature! breed of greatness!

4.2.24–25

This youth, howe'er distress'd, appears he hath had good
   ancestors.

4.2.47–48

How angel-like [you] sing!

4.2.48

HAMLET

To the celestial and my soul's idol, the most beautified [you].
2.2.109–10

I have an eye of you. If you love me, hold not off.
                                            2.2.290–91

What a piece of work [are you], how noble in reason,
    how infinite in faculties, in form and moving how
    express and admirable, in action how like an angel, in
    apprehension how like a god: the beauty of the world,
    the paragon of animals.
                                            2.2.303–7

Your lady-ship is nearer to heaven than when I saw you
    last.
                                            2.2.421–22

Your voice [is] like a piece of uncurrent gold.
                                            2.2.423–24

[You] please not the million, [you're] caviare to the
    general.
                                            2.2.432–33

[You are] as wholesome as sweet.
                                            2.2.440–41

[You are] by very much more handsome than fine.
                                            2.2.441

'Fore God, my lord, well spoken, with good accent and
    good discretion.
                                            2.2.462–63

O, what a noble mind.
                                            3.1.152

Blest are those whose blood and judgement are so
    commeddled.
                                            3.2.68–69

Give me that man
That is not passion's slave, and I will wear him
In my heart's core, ay, in my heart of heart,
As I do thee.

3.2.71–74

As you said—and wisely was it said.

3.3.30

What a grace [is] seated on [your] brow,
Hyperion's curls, the front of Jove himself,
An eye like Mars to threaten and command,
A station like the herald Mercury
New-lighted on a heaven-kissing hill,
A combination and a form indeed
Where every god [doth] seem to set his seal
To give the world assurance of a man.

3.4.55–62

[Your] worth, if praises may go back again,
Stood challenger on mount of all the age
For [your] perfections.

4.7.27–29

You have been talk'd of since your travel much
        . . . for a quality
Wherein they say you shine.

4.7.70–72

I know [you] well. [You are] the brooch indeed
And gem of all the nation.

4.7.92–93

[You are] a fellow of infinite jest, of most excellent fancy.

5.1.178–79

What a king is this!

5.2.62

In the verity of extolment, I take [you] to be a soul of
great article.

5.2.115–16

Your skill shall like a star i'th' darkest night
Stick fiery off indeed.

5.2.253–54

LOVE'S LABOUR'S LOST

Lord, how wise you are!

1.2.129

Nothing but fair is that which you inherit.

4.1.20

By heaven, that thou art fair, is most infallible; true, that
thou art beauteous; truth itself, that thou art lovely.
More fairer than fair, beautiful than beauteous, truer
than truth itself, have commiseration on thy heroical
vassal!

4.1.61–65

By heaven the wonder in a mortal eye! . . . as upright as
the cedar . . . as fair as day.

4.3.82,86,87

All hail, the richest beauties on the earth!

5.2.158

MEASURE FOR MEASURE

Heaven doth with [you] as we with torches do,
Not light them for themselves.

1.1.32–33

[You] will play with reason and discourse,
And well [you] can persuade.

1.2.175–76

I hold you as a thing enskied and sainted.

1.4.34

By your renouncement, [I hold you] an immortal spirit,
And to be talk'd with in sincerity,
As with a saint.

1.4.35–37

        You have the grace by your fair prayer
To soften [me].

1.4.69–70

I would to heaven I had your potency.

2.2.66

[You] play such fantastic tricks before high heaven
As makes the angels weep.

2.2.122–23

Thou'rt i' th' right, girl; more o' that.

2.2.130

[You] put mettle in restrained means.

2.4.48

With an outstretch'd throat I'll tell the world aloud
What man thou art.

                    2.4.152–53

Yet hath [you] in [you] a mind of honour.

                    2.4.178

[You] are as all comforts are: most good, most good
    indeed.

                    3.1.55

The hand that hath made you fair hath made you good.
                    3.1.179–80

Grace, being the soul of your complexion, shall keep the
    body of it ever fair.

                    3.1.182–83

[You] draw with idle spiders' strings
Most ponderous and substantial things!
                    3.2.268–69

[Your] advice hath often still'd my brawling discontent.
                    4.1.8–9

I do constantly believe you.

                    4.1.21

There is written in your brow, . . . honesty and
    constancy; if I read it not truly, my ancient skill
    beguiles me.

                    4.2.152–54

O my dear lord, I crave no other, nor no better man.
                    5.1.423–24

The Merry Wives of Windsor

I know [this] young gentlewoman; [you] have good gifts.

1.1.56

[You are] a region in Guiana, all gold and bounty.

1.3.64–65

Surely, I think you have charms, la; yes, in truth.

2.2.98–99

Let the court of France show me such another [like
    you].

3.3.48

I see how thine eye would emulate the diamond.

3.3.48–49

Thou hast the right arched beauty of the brow that
    becomes the ship-tire, the tire-valiant, or any tire of
    Venetian admittance.

3.3.49–52

What made me love thee? Let that persuade thee there's
    something extraordinary in thee.

3.3.62–63

Albeit I will confess thy father's wealth
Was the first motive that I woo'd thee . . .
Yet, wooing thee, I found thee of more value
Than stamps in gold or sums in sealed bags;
And 'tis the very riches of thyself
That now I am at.

3.4.13–18

A kind heart [you] hath: a woman would run through
   fire and water for such a kind heart.

3.4.99–100

I like [your] money well.

3.5.53

'Tis one of the best discretions of a 'oman as ever I did
   look upon.

4.4.1–2

A MIDSUMMER NIGHT'S DREAM

The wildest hath not such a heart as you.
2.1.229

Happy is [my lady], wheresoe'er she lies,
For she hath blessed and attractive eyes.
2.2.89–90

How came [your] eyes so bright?
2.2.91

I pray thee, gentle mortal, sing again:
Mine ear is much enamour'd of thy note;
So is mine eye enthralled to thy shape;
And thy fair virtue's force perforce doth move me
On the first view to say, to swear, I love thee.
3.1.132–36

Thou art as wise as thou art beautiful.
3.1.142

[You are] the object and the pleasure of mine eye.
4.1.169

[You are] the fairest dame
That liv'd, that lov'd, that lik'd, that look'd with cheer.
5.1.282–83

Thy sweet eyes.
These lily lips,
This cherry nose,
These yellow cowslip cheeks
5.1.316–19

MUCH ADO ABOUT NOTHING

Come, come, do you think I do not know you by your
excellent wit? Can virtue hide itself?
2.1.111–112

OTHELLO

Another of [your] fathom [there is] none.
1.1.150

[You're] a proper man.
1.3.391

[You] paragon description and wild fame;
[You] excel the quirks of blazoning pens
And in th'essential vesture of creation
Do tire [the Creator].
2.1.62–65

Tempests themselves, high seas, and howling winds,
The guttered rocks and congregated sands, . . .
As having sense of beauty, do omit
Their mortal natures, letting [you] go safely by.
2.1.68–72

[You are] ever fair and never proud,
[You have] tongue at will, and yet [are] never loud.
2.1.148–49

Very good, well kissed, and excellent courtesy: 'tis so
indeed!
2.1.174–75

O my fair warrior!
2.1.180

[You are] full of most blest condition.
2.1.247–48

O, the world hath not a sweeter creature: [you] might lie
by an emperor's side and command him tasks.
4.1.180–82

O, [you] will sing the savageness out of a bear! of so high
and plenteous wit and invention!
4.1.185–87

[Your skin is] smooth as monumental alabaster.
5.2.5

Thou [art the] cunning'st pattern of excelling nature.
5.2.11

[You are] great of heart.
5.2.359

PERICLES

Nature this dowry gave: to glad [your] presence,
The senate-house of planets all did sit
To knit in [you] their best perfections.
1.1.10–12

[You] come apparell'd like the spring,
Graces [your] subjects, and [your] thoughts the king
Of every virtue [which] gives renown to men!
1.1.13–15

Heaven, that I had thy head!
1.1.110

Sit down; thou art no flatterer;
I thank thee for't
1.2.60–61

Thy wisdom makes a prince thy servant,
What would'st thou have me do?
1.2.64–65

I [seek] the purchase of a glorious beauty,
From whence an issue I might propagate.
1.2.72–73

To me [you] seem like diamond to glass.
2.3.36

I do
Protest my ears were never better fed
With such delightful pleasing harmony.
2.5.26–28

[You have] gain'd
Of education all the grace,

Which makes [you] both the heart and place
Of general wonder.

4.Chorus.8–11

[Your] fingers are long, small, white as milk.

4.Chorus.22

When to th'lute [you sang, you] made the night-bird
mute.

4.Chorus.25–26

Out of thy long-experienc'd time
Give me some present counsel.

4.1.60–61

[You are] a goodly creature.

4.1.9

You are well favour'd, and your looks forshow
You have a gentle heart.

4.1.85–86

[You have] a good face, speak well, and have excellent
good clothes.

4.2.44–45

Come, the gods have done their part in you.

4.2.66

When nature fram'd this piece, she meant thee a good
turn.

4.2.137–38

What a paragon [you are].

4.2.138

You make the judgement good
That thought you worthy of it.

                    4.6.92–93

Had I brought hither a corrupted mind,
Thy speech had alter'd it.

                    4.6.103–4

Thou art a piece of virtue.

                    4.6.111

[You], . . . with [your] sweet harmony
And other chosen attractions, would allure,
And make a batt'ry through [my] deafen'd ports,
Which now are midway stopp'd.

                    5.1.44–47

Fair one, [you are] all goodness that consists in beauty.
                    5.1.70

[You are] wand-like straight.

                    5.1.109

[You are] silver-voic'd.

                    5.1.110

[Your] eyes [are] jewel-like and cas'd . . . richly.
                    5.1.110–11

I'll hear you more, to th' bottom of your story,
And never interrupt you.

                    5.1.164–65

I will believe you by the syllable.

                    5.1.167

[Thou art] most wise in general.

                              5.1.182

Thou hast been godlike perfect.

                              5.1.206

The gods can have no mortal officer
More like a god than you.

                         5.3.62–63

ROMEO AND JULIET

She's fair I love.

                              1.1.204

In strong proof of chastity [you are] well arm'd
From love's weak childish bow [you] live uncharm'd.

                              1.1.208–9

[You are] the hopeful lady of my earth.

                              1.2.15

[You are] a virtuous and well-govern'd youth.

                              1.5.66

You are a saucy boy.

                              1.5.82

[You're] a good lady, and a wise and virtuous [one].

                              1.5.113

Retain that dear perfection, which [you own]
Without [a] title.

                         2.2.46–47

[Your] face be better than any man's, yet [your] leg
   excels all men's, and for a hand and a foot and a body,
   though they be not to be talked on, yet they are past
   compare.

2.5.40–43

[You are] the flower of courtesy.

2.5.43

[Imagination] more rich in matter than in words
Brags of [your] substance, not of ornament.

2.6.30–31

Every tongue that speaks
But [your] name speaks heavenly eloquence.

3.2.32–33

Upon [your] brow shame is asham'd to sit,
For 'tis a throne where honour may be crown'd
Sole monarch of the universal earth.

3.2.92–94

O lord, I could have stay'd here all the night
To hear good counsel. O, what learning is.

3.3.158–59

THE TAMING OF THE SHREW

In [your] silence do I see
Maid's mild behaviour and sobriety.

1.1.70–71

I saw sweet beauty in [your] face.

1.1.167

I saw [your] coral lips to move,
And with [your] breath [you] did perfume the air.
Sacred and sweet was all I saw in [you].

1.1.174–76

I am a gentleman . . .
That hearing of [your] beauty and [your] wit,
[Your] affability and bashful modesty,
[Your] wondrous qualities and mild behaviour,
Am bold to show myself a forward guest
Within your house, to make mine eye the witness
Of that report which I so oft have heard.

2.1.47–53

[You] sing as sweetly as a nightingale.

2.1.171

I'll commend [your] volubility,
And say [you] uttereth piercing eloquence.

2.1.175–76

Hearing thy mildness prais'd in every town,
Thy virtues spoke of, and thy beauty sounded,
Yet not so deeply as to thee belongs,
Myself am mov'd to woo thee for my wife.

2.1.191–94

I find you passing gentle.
'Twas told me you were rough, and coy, and sullen,
And now I find report a very liar;
For thou art pleasant, gamesome, passing courteous,
But slow in speech, yet sweet as spring-time flowers.
Thou canst not frown, thou canst not look askance,
Nor bite the lip, as angry wenches will,
Nor hast thou pleasure to cross in talk.
But thou with mildness entertain'st thy wooers,

With gentle conference, soft and affable.
Why does the world report that [thou] doth limp?
O slanderous world! [Thou] like the hazel-twig
[Art] straight and slender, and as brown in hue
As hazel-nuts and sweeter than the kernels.
O, let me see thee walk. Thou dost not halt.

2.1.236–50

For [you're] not froward, but modest as the dove.
[You] are not hot, but temperate as the morn.
For patience [you] will prove a second Grissel,
And Roman Lucrece for [your] chastity.

2.1.285–89

THE TEMPEST

I have great comfort from this fellow.

1.1.28

[This] touch'd the very virtue of compassion in thee.

1.2.26–27

[You are] a piece of virtue.

1.2.56

Your tale, sir, would cure deafness.

1.2.106

　　　I might call him
A thing divine; for nothing natural
I ever saw so noble.

1.2.420–22

Most sure the goddess on whom these airs attend!

1.2.424–25

                              This
Is the third man that e'er I saw; the first
That e'er I sigh'd for.
                                        1.2.447–49

What impossible matter will [you] make easy next?
                                        2.1.85

You are [a gentleman] of brave mettle.
                                        2.1.175

[I'll] follow thee, thou wondrous man.
                                        2.2.163–64

The mistress which I serve quickens what's dead,
And makes my labours pleasures.
                                        3.1.6–7

                              O, she is
Ten times more gentle than her father's crabbed,
And he's compos'd of harshness.
                                        3.1.7–9

Precious creature.
                                        3.1.25

Indeed the top of admiration! worth
What's dearest to the world!
                                        3.1.38–39

              Full many a lady
I have ey'd with best regard, and many a time
Th'harmony of their tongues hath into bondage
Brought my too diligent ear: for several virtues
Have I lik'd several women; never any
With so full soul, but some defect in her
Did quarrel with the noblest grace she ow'd,

And put it to the foil: but you, O you,
So perfect and so peerless, are created
Of every creature's best.

3.1.39–48

[You] outstrip all praise,
And make it halt behind [you].

4.1.10–11

TROILUS AND CRESSIDA

[You] looked yesternight fairer than ever I saw [you]
    look, or any woman else.

1.1.32–33

[You] would be as fair o' Friday as Helen is on Sunday.

1.1.76–77

[Your] bed is India; there [you] lie, a pearl.

1.1.100

I think [your] smiling becomes [you] better than any
    man in all Phrygia.

1.2.124–25

O, [you] smile valiantly.

1.2.126

[You] have a shrewd wit, I can tell you, and [you're] a
    man good enough.

1.2.192–93

Look how [you] look, there's a countenance: is't not a
    brave man?

1.2.203–4

[You are] the mortal Venus, the heart-blood of beauty,
   love's visible soul.

                       3.1.31–32

[You are] full of harmony.

                       3.1.52

By my troth, sweet lord, thou hast a fine forehead.

                       3.1.102–3

O that I thought it could be in a woman—
As, if it can, I will presume in you—
To feed for aye her lamp and flames of love;
To keep her constancy in plight and youth,
Outliving beauty's outward, with a mind
That doth renew swifter than blood decays!

                       3.2.156–61

[You are like] the Grecian youths . . . full of quality,
Their loving well compos'd, with gift of nature flowing,
And swelling o'er with arts and exercise.

                       4.4.74–76

[You are] a woman of quick sense.

                       4.5.54

TWELFTH NIGHT

O, when mine eyes did see [you] first,
Methought [you] purg'd the air of pestilence;
That instant was I turn'd into a hart,
And my desires, like fell and cruel hounds,
E'er since pursue me.

                       1.1.19–23

I will believe thou hast a mind that suits
With this thy fair and outward character.

1.2.50–51

I'll drink to [you] as long as there is a passage in my
throat.

1.3.38–39

Most radiant, exquisite, and unmatchable beauty!

1.5.171–72

'Tis beauty truly blent, whose red and white
Nature's own sweet and cunning hand laid on.

1.5.242–43

I suppose [you] virtuous, know [you] noble,
Of great estate, of fresh and stainless youth;
In voices well divulg'd, free, learn'd, and valiant,
And in dimension, and the shape of nature
A gracious person.

1.5.262–66

Thy tongue, thy face, thy limbs, actions, and spirit
Do give thee five-fold blazon.

1.5.296–97

Methinks I feel this youth's perfections
With an invisible and subtle stealth
To creep in at mine eyes.

1.5.300–2

I do I know not what, and fear to find
Mine eye too great a flatterer for my mind.
Fate, show thy force; ourselves we do not owe.
What is decreed, must be: and be this so.

1.5.315

[You bear] a mind that envy could not but call fair.
2.1.28–29

Before me, [you're] a good wench.
2.3.178

My love, more noble than the world,
Prizes not quantity of dirty lands;
The parts that fortune hath bestow'd upon [you],
. . . I hold as giddily as fortune:
But 'tis that miracle and queen of gems
That nature pranks [you] in, attracts my soul.
2.4.81–87

The Two Gentlemen of Verona

Of many good, I think [you] best.
1.2.21

[Your] beauty is exquisite, but [your] favour infinite.
2.1.52–53

I have loved [you] ever since I saw [you], and still I see
[you] beautiful.
2.1.63–64

O excellent motion! O exceeding puppet!
2.1.89

A fine volley of words, [gentleman], and quickly shot off.
2.4.30

[You] made use and fair advantage of [your] days:
[Your] years but young, but [your] experience old;
[Your] head unmellow'd, but [your] judgment ripe;
And in a word (for far behind [your] worth

Comes all the praises that I now bestow)
[You are] complete in feature and in mind,
With all good grace to grace a gentleman.
                                        2.4.63–69

[You are] worthy for an empress' love
As meet to be an emperor's counsellor.
                                        2.4.71–72

[You are] not a heavenly saint . . . but . . . an earthly
    paragon.
                                        2.4.140–41

        If not divine,
Yet . . . be a principality,
Sovereign to all the creatures on the earth.
                                        2.4.146–48

        All I can is nothing
To [you] whose worth makes other worthies nothing:
[you] alone.
                                        2.4.160–62

'Tis but [your] picture I have yet beheld,
And that hath dazzled my reason's light;
But when I look on [your] perfections,
There is no reason but I shall be blind.
                                        2.4.205–8

Base men . . . use [oaths] to so base effect;
But truer stars did govern [your] birth,
[Your] words are bonds, [your] oaths are oracles,
[Your] love sincere, [your] thoughts immaculate,
[Your] tears pure messengers sent from [your] heart,
[Your] heart as far from fraud as heaven from earth.
                                        2.7.73–78

[You are] too fair, too true, too holy,
To be corrupted with my worthless gifts.

4.2.5–6

Thou art a gentleman
(Think not I flatter, for I swear I do not)
Valiant, wise, remorseful, well accomplish'd.

4.3.11–13

I do applaud thy spirit . . .
And think thee worthy of an empress' love.

5.4.138–39

THE WINTER'S TALE

Let what is dear in Sicily be cheap.
Next to thyself.

1.2.175–76

Though I am not bookish, yet I can read waiting-
gentlewoman in the scape.

3.3.72–73

[There was] never . . . a piece of beauty rarer.

4.4.32

This is the prettiest low-born lass that ever
Ran on the green-sward.

4.4.156–57

Nothing [you] do or seem
But smacks of something greater than [your]self,
Too noble for this place.

4.4.157–59

[You are] the queen of curds and cream.

4.4.161

[You] dance featly.

4.4.178

How prettily the young swain seems to wash
The hand was fair before!

4.4.367–68

    I cannot speak
So well, nothing so well; no, nor mean better:
By th' pattern of mine own thoughts I cut out
The purity of [yours].

4.4.381–84

    [You are] the sweet'st companion that e'er man
Bred his hopes out of.

4.4.11–12

If, one by one, I wedded all the world,
Or from the all that are took something good,
To make a perfect woman, [you]
Would be unparallel'd.

5.1.13–16

[You are] the fairest I have yet beheld.

5.1.87

    [You are] the most peerless piece of earth, I think,
That e'er the sun shone bright on.

5.1.94–95

    [You have] not been,
Nor was not to be equall'd.

5.1.100–1

        This is a creature,
Would she begin a sect, might quench the zeal
Of all professors else; make proselytes
Of who she but bid follow.

5.1.106–9

Women will love [you], that [you are] a woman
More worth than any man; men, that [you are]
The rarest of all women.

5.1.110–12

        O royal piece!
There's magic in thy majesty.

5.3.38–39

Fast-talking

SEDUCTIONS OFTEN MEET OBSTRUCTIONS. Shakespeare surmounts them, surrounds them, subverts them in all sorts of ways, but one surefire technique is sheer exhilaration by acceleration. Get ahead of the game. Flummox your quarry with confusion and stay *way* ahead.

Touchstone baffles Audry into bed. She barely knows what's happening. Rosaline has big, strong Orlando obeying orders and making no excuses in the woods. How does she do it? She throws him off balance with pure bravado, and keeps him off balance till she has her way. She even makes him show up on time to receive his treatment.

Fast-talking overwhelms with glib, plausible nonsense. Sometimes it's false, but of course we recommend a flurry of truth. The language skims the surface, makes rash assumptions, presumes to know what's best for someone else. The logic leaps from non-argument to non-argument. It leaves room for hearing what isn't quite said, without leaving time for reflection. It's slippery, it's slimy, it's seductive. (That slip past you? That's fast-talking.)

At its loveliest, fast-talking is a sparkling cascade of wit as you slyly reveal what you really desire. You take the initiative in a passionate cause, a preemptive refusal of any refusal. It's exciting, exhilarating, exhausting. The ride makes you more beautiful than ever, even if you were passable to begin with. Your quarry is reduced to helplessness, and they think they're delighted to be. These pages lay out Shakespearean answers that throw questioners into doubt and put questions to rout.

ALL'S WELL THAT ENDS WELL

There's little can be said in't; 'tis against the rule of
nature. To speak on the part of virginity is to accuse
your mothers, which is most infallible disobedience.
He that hangs himself is a virgin; virginity murthers
itself, and should be buried in highways out of all
sanctified limit, as a desperate offendress against
nature.

1.1.133–39

Besides, virginity is peevish, proud, idle, made of self-love
which is the most inhibited sin in the canon. Keep it
not; you cannot choose but lose by't. Out with't!
Within the year it will make itself two, which is a
goodly increase, and the principal itself not much the
worse. Away with't!

1.1.141–46

    Come, come, disclose
The state of your affection, for your passions
Have to the full appeach'd.

1.3.185

    If thou proceed
As high as word, my deed shall match thy deed.

2.1.208–9

Will your answer serve fit to all questions?

2.2.19

It must be an answer of most monstrous size that must
fit all demands.

2.2.31–32

If I should swear by Jove's great attributes
I lov'd you dearly, would you believe my oaths
When I did love you ill?

4.2.25–27

As You Like It

Hereafter, in a better world than this,
I shall desire more love and knowledge of you.

1.2.274–75

In thy youth thou wast as true a lover
As ever sigh'd upon a midnight pillow.

2.4.23–24

If thy love were ever like to mine,
As sure I think did never man love so,
How many actions most ridiculous
Hast thou been drawn to by thy fantasy?

2.4.25–28

We that are true lovers run into strange capers; but as all
   is mortal in nature, so is all nature in love mortal in
   folly.

2.4.51–53

That they call compliment is like th'encounter of two
   dog-apes.

2.5.23–24

When a man thanks me heartily, methinks I have given
   him a penny and he renders me the beggarly thanks.

2.5.24–26

It is as easy to count atomies as to resolve the
  propositions of a lover.
                          3.2.228–29

[If there's no clock in this forest] then there is no true
  lover in the forest, else sighing every minute and
  groaning every hour would detect the lazy foot of
  Time, as well as a clock.
                          3.2.297–99

Her that you love [is apter] to believe it, than to confess
  she does. That is one of the points in the which
  women still give the lie to their consciences.
                          3.2.377–81

The reason why [those mad with love] are not so
  punished and cured is that the lunacy is so ordinary
  that the whippers are in love too.
                          3.2.390–93

I [set my suitor] every day to woo me. At which time
  would I, being but a moonish youth, grieve, be
  effeminate, changeable, longing and liking, proud,
  fantastical, apish, shallow, inconstant, full of tears, full
  of smiles, for every passion something and for no
  passion truly anything, as boys and women are for
  the most part cattle of this colour; would now like
  him, now loathe him; then entertain him, then
  forswear him; now weep for him, then spit at him;
  that I drave my suitor from his mad humour of love
  to a living humour of madness, which was, to
  forswear the full stream of the world and to live in a
  nook merely monastic. And thus I cured him.
                          3.2.397–409

The truest poetry is the most feigning, and lovers are
    given to poetry.

                    3.3.16–17

Honesty coupled to beauty is to have honey a sauce to
    sugar.

                    3.3.26–27

Praised be the gods for thy foulness; sluttishness may
    come hereafter. But be it as it may be, I will marry
    thee.

                    3.3.34–36

I were better to be married of [this priest] than another,
    for he is not like to marry me well; and not being well
    married, it will be a good excuse for me hereafter to
    leave my wife.

                    3.3.81–85

Now counterfeit to swoon: why now fall down,
Or if thou canst not, O for shame, for shame,
Lie not, to say mine eyes are murderers.

                    3.5.17–19

Think not I love [you], though I ask for [you].
                    3.5.109

[You are] not very tall, yet for [your] years [you're] tall.
[Your] leg is but so so; and yet 'tis well.

                    3.5.118–19

For my part I love [you] not, nor hate [you] not.
                    3.5.126–27

           And yet
I have more cause to hate [you] than to love [you].

                    3.5.128

You were better speak first, and when you were gravelled
   for lack of matter, you might take occasion to kiss.
                            4.1.70–72

        For lovers lacking—God
warr'nt us!—matter, the cleanliest shift is to kiss.
How if the kiss be denied?
Then [you] put [me] to entreaty, and there begins new
matter.
                            4.1.73–77

Make the doors upon a woman's wit, and it will out at
   the casement; shut that, and 'twill out at the keyhole;
   stop that, 'twill fly with the smoke out at the
   chimney.
                            4.1.153–56

My affection hath an unknown bottom like the Bay of
   Portugal. As fast as [I] pour affection in, it runs out.
                            4.1.197–200

That same wicked bastard of Venus, that was begot of
   thought, conceived of spleen and born of madness,
   that blind rascally boy that abuses everyone's eyes
   because his own are out, let him be judge of how deep
   I am in love.
                            4.1.201–5

'Twas I. But 'tis not I. I do not shame
To tell you what I was, since my conversion
So sweetly tastes, being the thing I am.
                            4.3.135–37

Give me your hand . . .
Then learn this of me. To have is to have.
                            5.1.37–39

I am . . . he sir that must marry this woman. Therefore
    you clown, abandon—which is in the vulgar leave—
    the society—which in the boorish is company—of
    this female—which in the common is woman.
    Which together is, abandon the society of this
    female, or clown thou perishest; or to thy better
    understanding, diest; or, to wit, I kill thee, make thee
    away, translate thy life into death, thy liberty into
    bondage. I will deal in poison with thee, or in
    bastinado, or in steel. I will bandy with thee in
    faction; I will o'er-run thee with policy; I will kill thee
    a hundred and fifty ways. Therefore tremble and
    depart.

5.1.43–56

Whiles a wedlock hymn we sing,
[We'll] feed [ourselves] with questioning,
That reason wonder may diminish
How thus we met, and these things finish.

5.4.136–39

CYMBELINE

[I wish] I held this hand, whose touch
(Whose every touch) would force the feeler's soul
To th'oath of loyalty.

1.6.100–102

I know not why
I love this youth, and I have heard you say,
Love's reason's without reason.

4.2.20–22

HAMLET

You cannot speak of reason to [me]
And lose your voice.

1.2.44–45

[I would not] beteem the winds of heaven
Visit [your] face too roughly.

1.2.141–42

      If [you] say [you] love [me],
It fits [my] wisdom so far to believe it
as [you] in [your] particular act and place
May give [your] saying deed.

1.3.24–27

[Don't] keep you in the rear of your affection
Out of the shot and danger of desire.

1.3.34–35

In the morn and liquid dew of youth
Contagious blastments are most imminent.

1.3.41–42

You do not understand yourself so clearly.

1.3.96

I do not know . . . what I should think.

1.3.104

Nature cannot choose his origin.

1.4.26

[You] wax desperate with imagination.

1.4.87

If thou hast nature in thee, bear it not.

1.5.81

It is common for the younger sort
To lack discretion.

2.1.116–17

There is nothing either good or bad but thinking makes
it so.

2.2.249–50

[I] love [thee] passing well.

2.2.404

Use [me] after your own honour and dignity: the less
[I] deserve, the more merit is in your bounty.

2.2.525–27

What should a man do but be merry?

3.2.123–24

[You will] seem harsh awhile, but in the end accept [my]
love.

3.2.133 Stage Direction

'Tis a question left us yet to prove,
Whether love lead fortune or else fortune love.

3.2.197–98

Our thoughts are ours, their ends none of our own.

3.2.208

Lay not that flattering unction to your soul.

3.4.147

O heavens, is't possible a young maid's wits
Should be as mortal as an old man's life?
                                        4.5.159–60

Custom hath made ... [you] a property of easiness.
                                        5.1.67

[My] definement suffers no perdition in you, though I
    know to divide [me] inventorially would dozy
    th'arithmetic of memory.
                                        5.2.112–14

[Your] intrusion [is] of such dearth and rareness as, to
    make true diction of [you].
                                        5.2.117–18

LOVE'S LABOUR'S LOST

I will hereupon confess I am in love; and as it is base for
    a soldier to love, so am I in love with a base wench.
                                        1.2.53–54

If drawing my sword against the humour of affection
    would deliver me from the reprobate thought of it, I
    would take Desire prisoner, and ransom him to any
    French courtier for a new-devised courtesy.
                                        1.2.55–59

Shall I command thy love? I may. Shall I enforce thy love?
    I could. Shall I entreat thy love? I will.
                                        4.1.80–82

But that you take what doth to you belong,
It were a fault to snatch words from my tongue.
                                        5.2.381–82

Our love being yours, the error that love makes
Is likewise yours.

5.2.763–64

MEASURE FOR MEASURE

Believe not that the dribbling dart of love
Can pierce a complete bosom.

1.3.2–3

Some rise by sin, and some by virtue fall.

2.1.38

      Go to your bosom,
Knock there, and ask your heart what it doth know.

2.2.137–38

      Can it be
That modesty may more betray our sense
Than woman's lightness?

2.2.168–70

Women?—Help, heaven! Men their creation mar
In profiting by them. Nay, call us ten times frail;
For we are soft as our complexions are,
And credulous to false prints.

2.4.126–29

      Be that you are,
That is, a woman; if you be more, you're none.

2.4.133–34

[I have fallen] by prompture of the blood.

2.4.177

Think you I can a resolution fetch
From flowery tenderness?

3.1.81–82

The assault that [I have] made to you . . . frailty hath
    examples for [my] falling.

3.1.183–85

Love talks with better knowledge, and knowledge with
    dearer love.

3.2.146–47

Come, sir, I know what I know.

3.2.148

There is so great a fever on goodness that the dissolution
    of it must cure it.

3.2.216–17

Craft against vice I must apply.

3.2.270

        Music oft hath such a charm
To make bad good, and good provoke to harm.
                                    4.1.14–15

Put not yourself into amazement how these things
    should be; all difficulties are but easy when they are
    known.

4.2.203–5

It is ten times true, for truth is truth
To th'end of reck'ning.

5.1.48–49

[Your] act did not o'ertake [your] bad intent,
And must be buried but as an intent
That perish'd by the way.

5.1.449–51

The Merry Wives of Windsor

I beseech you be ruled by your well-willers.

1.1.63–64

I will marry [you] upon any reasonable demands.

1.1.206–7

Ask me no reason why I love you.

2.1.4

Though Love use Reason for his precisian, he admits
  him not for his counsellor.

2.1.4–6

You are not young, no more am I; go to, then, there's
  sympathy.

2.1.6–7

You are merry, so am I; ha, ha, then, there's more
  sympathy.

2.1.7–8

You love sack, and so do I; would you desire better
  sympathy?

2.1.8–9

[I have] not only bought many presents to give [you]
  but have given largely to many to know what [you]
  would have given.

2.2.192–94

Heaven knows how I love you, and you shall one day
   find it.

                              3.3.74–75

[I love you] as well as I love any woman in
   Gloucestershire.

                              3.4.43–44

I see you are obsequious in your love, and I profess
   requital to a hair's breadth, not only . . . in the simple
   office of love, but in all the accoutrement,
   complement, and ceremony of it.

                              4.2.2–5

A Midsummer Night's Dream

Ay me! For aught that I could ever read,
Could ever hear by take or history,
The course of true love never did run smooth.

                              1.1.132–34

Things base and vile, holding no quantity,
Love can transpose to form and dignity:
Love looks not with the eyes, but with the mind,
And therefore is wing'd Cupid painted blind;
Nor hath Love's mind of any judgement taste:
Wings, and no eyes, figure unheedy haste.
And therefore is Love said to be a child,
Because in choice he is so oft beguil'd
As waggish boys, in game, themselves forswear,
So the boy Love is perjur'd everywhere.

                              1.1.232–41

If then true lovers have been ever cross'd,
It stands as an edict in destiny.

1.1.150–51

      If thou lov'st me then,
Steal forth thy father's house tomorrow night;
And in the wood, a league without the town . . .
There will I stay for thee.

1.1.163–68

Who will not change a raven for a dove?
The will of man is by his reason sway'd,
And reason says you are the worthier maid.

2.2.113–15

What thou seest when thou dost wake,
Do it for thy true love take;
Love and languish for his sake.

3.2.26–28

Why should you think that I should woo in scorn?
Scorn and derision never come in tears.
Look when I vow, I weep; and vows so born,
In their nativity all truth appears.

3.2.122–25

How can these things in me seem scorn to you,
Bearing the badge of faith to prove them true?

3.2.126–27

Look where thy love comes; yonder is thy dear.

3.2.176

I have had a most rare vision. I have had a dream, past
    the wit of man to say what dream it was.

4.1.203–5

The eye of man hath not heard, the ear of man hath not
    seen, man's hand is not able to taste, his tongue to
    conceive, nor his heart to report, what my dream was.
                                              4.1.209–12

Lovers and madmen have such seething brains,
Such shaping fantasies, that apprehend
More than cool reason ever comprehends.
                                              5.1.4–6

Trust me, sweet.

                                              5.1.99

MUCH ADO ABOUT NOTHING

He that hath a beard is more than a youth, and he that
    hath no beard is less than a man; and he that is more
    than a youth is not for me; and he that is less than a
    man I am not for him.
                                              2.1.32–35

Would it not grieve a woman to be overmastered with a
    piece of valiant dust, to make an account of her life to
    a clod of wayward marl?
                                              2.1.56–58

It were as possible for me to say I loved nothing so well
    as you, but believe me not; and yet I lie not; I confess
    nothing, nor I deny nothing.
                                              4.1.268–71

OTHELLO

[I'll] out-tongue [your] complaints.

                                              1.2.19

If [you have] a friend that loves [me],
[You] should teach him how to tell [your] story
And that would woo [me].

1.3.165–67

Confess that [you were] half the wooer.

1.3.174

But words are words.

1.3.219

What should I do? I confess it is my shame to be so
    fond, but it is not in my virtue to amend it.

1.3.318–19

[We are] as prime as goats, as hot as monkeys,
As salt as wolves in pride, and fools as gross
As ignorance made drunk.

3.3.406–8

Let us be wary, let us hide our loves.

3.3.422

There's millions now alive
That nightly lie in those unproper beds
Which they dare swear peculiar.

4.1.67–69

I grant indeed [that] your suspicion is not without wit
    and judgement.

4.2.212–13

[My sins] are loves I bear to you.

5.2.40

[I am] one that loved not wisely, but too well.

5.2.342

PERICLES

Who makes the fairest show means most deceit.

> 1.4.75

> [You] get
> All praises, which are paid as debts,
> And not as given.

> 4.Chorus.33–35

> Let not . . . flaming love thy bosom
> Enslave too nicely.

> 4.1.4–6

Come you're a young foolish sapling, and must be bow'd
    as I would have you.

> 4.2.83–85

[Your modesty] dignifies the renown of a bawd no less
    than it gives a good report to a number to be chaste.

> 4.6.37–38

> [Are you] not a fair creature?
> Faith, [you] would serve after a long voyage at sea.

> 4.6.41–42

> Truth can never be confirm'd enough,
> Though doubts did ever sleep.

> 5.1.201–2

ROMEO AND JULIET

> I have lost myself, I am not here.
> This is not [me], he's some other where.

> 1.1.195–96

O teach me how I should forget to think.

1.1.224

Let two more summers wither in their pride
Ere [you] may think [me] ripe to be a bride.

1.2.10–11

[To marry you] is an honour that I dream not of.

1.3.66

Is love a tender thing? It is too rough,
Too rude, too boisterous, and it pricks like thorn.

1.4.25–26

Dreamers often lie.

1.4.51

[You were] too early seen unknown, and known too late.

1.5.138

Cry but 'Ay me!' Pronounce but 'love' and 'dove',
Speak to my gossip Venus one fair word.

2.1.10–11

Why, is not this better now than groaning for love? Now
    art thou sociable.

2.4.88–89

Now art thou what thou art, by art as well as by nature.

2.4.90–91

A lover may bestride the gossamer
That idles in the wanton summer air
And yet not fall; so light is vanity.

2.6.18–20

Have done: some grief shows much of love,
But much of grief shows still some want of wit.

3.5.72–73

THE TAMING OF THE SHREW

Fair Leda's daughter had a thousand wooers,
Then well one more may fair Bianca have.

1.2.242–43

Hic ibat, as I told you before—*Simois*, I am Lucentio—
   hic est, son unto Vincentio of Pisa—*Sigeia tellus*,
   disguised thus to get your love—*Hic steterat*, and that
   Lucentio that comes a wooing—*Priami*, is my man
   Tranio—*regia*, bearing my port—*celsa senis*, that we
   might beguile the old pantaloon.

3.1.31–36

Now let me see if I can construe it: *Hic ibat Simois*, I
   know you not—*hic est Sigeia tellus*, I trust you not—
   Hic steterat Priami, take heed he hear us not—*regia*,
   presume not—*celsa senis*, despair not.

3.1.40–43

THE TEMPEST

I will be correspondent to command,
And do my spriting gently.

1.2.297–98

   What is't? a spirit?
Lord, how it looks about! Believe me, . . .
It carries a brave form. But 'tis a spirit.

1.2.412–14

O, that you bore
The mind that I do! what a sleep were this
For your advancement! Do you understand me?
                                    2.1.261–63

Hush, and be mute, or else our spell is marr'd.
                                    4.1.126–27

TROILUS AND CRESSIDA

This is the monstrosity in love, lady: that the will is
    infinite, and the execution confined: that the desire is
    boundless, and the act a slave to limit.
                                    3.2.79–82

You are wise,
Or else you love not; for to be wise and love
Exceeds man's might: that dwells with gods above.
                                    3.2.154–55

I do not call your faith in question
So mainly as my merit: I cannot sing,
Nor heel the high lavolt, nor sweeten talk,
Nor play at subtle games—fair virtues all,
To which the Grecians are most prompt and pregnant;
But I can tell that in each grace of these
There lurks a still and dumb-discoursive devil
That tempts most cunningly. But be not tempted.
                                    4.4.83–90

O beauty, where is thy faith?
                                    5.2.67

There is a credence in my heart,
An esperance so obstinately strong,
that doth invert th'attest of eyes and ears,
As if those organs had deceptious functions,
Created only to calumniate.

5.2.119–23

TWELFTH NIGHT

What else may hap, to time I will commit;
Only shape thou thy silence to my wit.

1.2.60–61

You must confine yourself within the modest limits of
    order.

1.3.8–9

You do usurp yourself: for what is yours to bestow is not
    yours to reserve.

1.5.188–90

O, such love
Could be but recompens'd, though you were crown'd
The nonpareil of beauty!

1.5.256–58

That's a degree to love.

3.1.125

I would you were as I would have you be.

3.1.144

Yet come again: for thou perhaps mayst move
That heart which now abhors, to like his love.

3.1.165–66

THE TWO GENTLEMEN OF VERONA

Since thou lov'st, love still, and thrive therein,
Even as I would, when I to love begin.
1.1.9–10

If [love is] haply won, perhaps a hapless gain;
If lost, why then a grievous labour won.
1.1.32–33

I have no other but a woman's reason:
I think [you] so, because I think [you] so.
1.2.23–24

To plead for love deserves more fee than hate.
1.2.48

You are metamorphosed with a mistress, that when I
look on you, I can hardly think you my master.
2.1.29–31

These follies [of being in love] are within you, and shine
through you like the water in an urinal.
2.1.37–38

In conclusion, I stand affected to [you].
2.1.80

If it please you, so; if not, why, so.
2.1.124

[You] sue to [me]; and [I have] taught [my] suitor,
[You] being [my] pupil, to become [my] tutor.
2.1.130–31

What, gone without a word?
Ay, so true love should do: it cannot speak,
For truth hath better deeds than words to grace it.

2.2.16–18

[I] borrow [my] wit from your ladyship's looks, and
  spend what [I] borrow kindly in your company.

2.4.35–36

To die is to be banish'd from myself,
And [you are] myself: banished from [you]
Is self from self. A deadly banishment.

3.1.171–73

He lives not now that knows me to be in love, yet I am
  in love, but a team of horse shall not pluck that from
  me; nor who 'tis I love; and yet 'tis a woman; but
  what woman I will not tell myself.

3.1.263–67

[You have] more qualities than a water-spaniel, which is
  much in a bare Christian.

3.1.269–71

[You have] many nameless virtues.

3.1.311

This discipline shows thou hast been in love.

3.2.86

The Winter's Tale

[You're] apparent to my heart.

1.2.177

I think you have
As little skill to fear as I have purpose
To put you to 't.

4.4.151–53

Goading and Prodding

WHEN YOUR QUARRY seems to lose interest, don't despair. You're lucky. You've got something to do. Get a grip on what you know they want, touch them with their own disinterest and veer them around. If the one you want is uncertain about you, try seeming uncertain about them. Sensing a new challenge, they just might perk up.

In Shakespeare's hands such situations became a whole theatrical career. And as you dabble in the human drama, you too can benefit from skepticism in the person you're seducing. It's your motivation. Without it there's no challenge, no edge, no achievement at the end—no excuse for failure. So if there's no play, look for someone else to play with.

When encountering doubt, you have to encourage your hesitating victim along. Excitement is what's needed, and prodding is a form of stimulation. Wind them up. Get them going. Here are lines that tease, mock, even insult. Make the one you want want to make things better with you. "We are wise girls," says the princess, "to mock our lovers so."

Serenity is overrated. It's an opiate that's always fatal to love. None of Shakespeare's big couples are calm. Passion is a long way from peace, yet cloying tranquility is where love tends to gravitate. The seducer has a job to do before boredom descends, before anyone gets set in their ways.

From the start you have to get a rise. So shake things up. Teasing shows interest. Torment is a form of affection. There's something sexy in someone with Trouble as a middle name.

ALL'S WELL THAT ENDS WELL

Unfold to us some warlike resistance.

1.1.114–15

Tell me thy reason why thou wilt marry.

1.2.25

More should I question thee, and more I must,
Though more to know could not be more to trust.

2.1.204–5

I think, sir, you can eat none of this homely meat.

2.2.44

Do you cry 'O Lord, sir!' at your whipping, and 'spare
not me'? Indeed your 'O Lord, sir!' is very sequent to
your whipping; you would answer very well to a
whipping, if you were but bound to't.

2.2.48–51

I play the noble housewife with the time,
To entertain it so merrily with a fool.

2.2.54–55

I'll like a maid the better whilst I have a tooth in my
head.

2.3.41–42

You do me most insupportable vexation.

2.3.227

[Your] promises, enticements, oaths, tokens, and all
these engines of lust, are not the things [you] go
under; many a maid hath been seduced by them; and
the misery is, example, that so terrible shows in the
wrack of maidenhood, cannot for all that dissuade

succession, but that [you] are limed with the twigs
that threaten [you].

3.5.18–24

This is the first truth that e'er thine own tongue was
guilty of.

4.1.32–33

Fair soul,
In your fine frame hath love no quality?

4.2.3–4

Be not so holy-cruel; love is holy.

4.2.32

Give me that ring.

4.2.39

I do presume, sir, that you are not fall'n
From the report that goes upon your goodness,
And therefore, goaded with most sharp occasions
Which lay nice manners by, I put you to
The use of your own virtues, for the which
I shall continue thankful.

5.2.12–17

Why do you look so strange upon your wife?

5. 3.167

ANTONY AND CLEOPATRA

If it be love indeed, tell me how much.

1.1.14

There's beggary in the love that can be reckoned.

1.1.15

I'll set a bourn how far to be beloved.

1.1.16

Now, for the love of Love and her soft hours,
Let's not confound the time with conference harsh.

1.1.45–46

[You are] cunning past man's thought.

1.2.152

Would I had never seen [you]!

1.2.159

       Oh, never was there queen
So mightily betrayed!

1.3.25–26

Why should I think you can be mine and true—
Though you in swearing shake the thronèd gods?

1.3.28–29

       Your honour calls you hence;
Therefore be deaf to my unpitied folly,
And all the gods go with you!

1.3.99–101

       I take no pleasure
In aught an eunuch has.

1.5.10–11

       When good will is showed, though't come too short,
The actor may plead pardon.

2.5.8–9

           I will betray
Tawny-finned fishes. My bended hook shall pierce
Their slimy jaws, and as I draw them up,

I'll think them every one [another you],
And say 'Ah, ha! You're caught!'

2.5.11–15

To try thy eloquence now 'tis time.

3.12.26

A woman is a dish for the gods if the devil dress her not.

5.2.273

As You Like It

You are too young in this.

1.1.54

I will not [let go of you] till I please: you shall hear me.

1.1.66

I see thou lov'st me not with the full weight that I love
thee.

1.2.7–8

Alas, [you are] too young. Yet [you] look successfully.

1.2.143

I beseech you, punish me not with your hard thoughts.

1.2.172–73

Where is this young gallant that is so desirous to lie
with his mother earth?

1.2.188–89

[You] lack then the love
Which teacheth thee that thou and I am one.
Shall we be sunder'd? Shall we part, sweet girl?

1.3.92–94

That is the way to make [me] scorn you still.

2.4.19

O thou didst then never love so heartily.
If thou remember'st not the slightest folly
That ever love did make thee run into.

2.4.30–32

Thou hast not loved
. . . if thou hast not broke from company
Abruptly as my passion now makes me.

2.4.36–38

I do not desire you to please me, I do desire you to sing.

2.5.15–16

[I would] put a man in [my] belly. [Are you] of God's
making? What manner of man? Is [your] head worth
a hat? Or [your] chin worth a beard?

3.2.201–3

[The marks of a lover are] a lean cheek, which you have
not; a blue eye and sunken, which you have not; an
unquestionable spirit, which you have not; a beard
neglected, which you have not . . . Then your hose
should be un-gartered, your bonnet unbanded, your
sleeve un-buttoned, your shoe untied, and everything
about you demonstrating a careless desolation. But
you are no such man: you are rather point-device in
your accoutrements, as loving yourself than seeming
the lover of any other.

3.2.363–74

Love is merely a madness, and I tell you, deserves as well
a dark house and a whip as madmen do.

3.2.388–89

What they do swear in poetry may be said as lovers they
do feign.

3.3.17–18

[Your] very hair is of the dissembling colour.

3.4.6

[Your] kisses are Judas's own children.

3.4.7–8

[Your] kissing is as full of sanctity as the touch of holy
bread.

3.4.12–13

[I have] bought a pair of cast lips of Diana. A nun of
winter's sisterhood kisses not more religiously, the
very ice of chastity is in them.

3.4.14–16

I think [you are] not a pick-purse nor a horse-stealer,
but for [your] verity of love, I do think [you] as
concave as a covered goblet or a worm-eaten nut.

3.4.21–23

The oath of a lover is no stronger than the word of a
tapster. They are both the confirmer of false
reckonings.

3.4.27–29

Thou tell'st me there is murder in mine eye:
'Tis pretty, sure, and very probable,
That eyes, that are the frail'st and softest things, . . .
Should be call'd tyrants, butchers, murderers.

3.5.10–14

Now I do frown on thee with all my heart,
And if mine eyes can wound, now let them kill thee.
                                    3.5.15–16

Though you have no beauty—
As by my faith I see no more in you
Than without candle may go dark to bed—
Must you be therefore proud and pitiless?
                                    3.5.37–40

No faith proud mistress, hope not after it.
                                    3.5.45

You foolish [creature], wherefore do you follow [me]
Like foggy South puffing with wind and rain?
                                    3.5.49–50

I must tell you friendly in your ear,
Sell when you can, you are not for all markets.
                                    3.5.59–60

I pray you do not fall in love with me,
For I am falser than vows made in wine.
Besides, I like you not.
                                    3.5.72–74

Omittance is no quittance.
I'll write to [you] a very taunting letter.
                                    3.5.133–34

I will be bitter with [you] and passing short.
                                    3.5.138

Where have you been all this while? You a lover! And
    you serve me such another trick, never come in my
    sight more.
                                    4.1.37–39

Break an hour's promise in love! He that will divide a
    minute into a thousand parts, and break but a part of
    the thousand part of a minute in the affairs of love, it
    may be said of him that Cupid hath clapped him o' th'
    shoulder, but I'll warrant him heart-whole.

4.1.42–47

[If] you be so tardy, come no more in my sight. I had as
    lief be wooed of a snail.

4.1.49–50

Who could be out [of things to say] being before his
    beloved mistress?
Marry that should you, if I were your mistress.

4.1.76–79

Now tell me how long you would have [me], after you
    have possessed [me]?

4.1.135–36

Men are April when they woo, December when they
    wed.

4.1.139–40

Maids are May when they are maids, but the sky changes
    when they are wives.

4.1.140–41

I will weep for nothing, like Diana in the fountain, and I
    will do that when you are disposed to be merry. I will
    laugh like a hyen, and that when thou art inclined to
    sleep.

4.1.145–48

By all oaths that are not dangerous, if you break one jot
    of your promise, or come one minute behind your
    hour, I will think you the most pathetical break-

promise, and the most hollow lover, and the most
unworthy of her you call [beloved], that may be
chosen out of the gross band of the unfaithful.

4.1.179–85

Beware my censure and keep your promise.

4.1.185–86

We must have your doublet and hose plucked over your
head, and show the world what the bird hath done to
her own nest.

4.1.192–94

[Your] love is not the hare that I do hunt;
Why write [you] so to me?

4.3.18–19

Come, come you are a fool,
And turn'd into the extremity of love.

4.3.22–23

Well, go your way to her, for I see love hath made thee a
tame snake.

4.3.69–70

There is too great testimony in your complexion that it
was a passion of earnest.

4.3.169–71

Take a good heart, and counterfeit to be a man.

4.3.173–74

You do love [me] so near the heart as your gesture cries
it out.

5.2.62–65

If sight and shape be true,
Why then my love adieu.

5.4.119–20

I will not eat my word; now thou art mine,
Thy faith my fancy to thee doth combine.

5.4.148–49

CYMBELINE

For my sake wear this,
It is a manacle of love, I'll place it
Upon this fairest prisoner.

1.2.52–54

[I] exceed in goodness the hugeness of your unworthy
   thinking.

1.5.141–42

Heavens know some men are much to blame.

1.7.76–77

I pray you, sir,
Deliver with more openness your answers
To my demands.

1.7.87–89

[Thou] solicits here a lady that disdains
Thee, and the devil alike.

1.7.147–48

I am much sorry, sir,
You put me to forget a lady's manners,
By being so verbal: and learn now, for all,

That I, which know my heart, do here pronounce,
By th' very truth of it, I care not for you.

2.3.103–7

That we two are asunder; let that grieve [you];
Some griefs are med'cinable, that is one of them,
For it doth physic love.

3.2.32–34

[Your] love-suit hath been to me
As fearful as a siege.

3.4.135–36

HAMLET

How is it that the clouds still hang on you?

1.2.66

[Your refusal is] a fault to heaven,
. . . a fault to nature,
To reason most absurd.

1.2.101–3

These blazes, . . .
Giving more light than heat, extinct in both
Even in their promise as it is a-making,
[I] must not take for fire.

1.3.117–20

    From this time
Be something scanter of [my] maiden presence.

1.3.120–22

[Your vows are] mere implorators of unholy suits,
Breathing like sanctified and pious bawds
The better to beguile.

1.3.129–31

[Do not] so slander any moment leisure
As to give words or talk with [me].

1.3.133–34

Hold off your hand.

1.4.80

O wicked wit, and gifts that have the power
So to seduce!

1.5.44–45

And so without more circumstance at all
I hold it fit that we shake hands and part,
You as your business and desire shall point you—
For every man hath business and desire,
Such as it is—and for my own poor part,
I will go pray.

1.5.133–38

Still your fingers on your lips.

1.5.195

    Put on [me]
What forgeries you please—marry, none so rank
As may dishonour [me]—. . .
But . . . such wanton, wild, and usual slips
As are companions noted and most known
To youth and liberty.

2.1.19–24

[I] close with you in this consequence.

2.1.46

You have me, have you not?

2.1.68

I [do] repel [your] letters and deny
[Your] access to me.

2.1.109–10

I fear'd [you] did but trifle
And meant to wrack [me]. But beshrew my jealousy!

2.1.112–13

Man delights not me—nor woman neither, though by
your smiling you seem to say so.

2.2.309–10

The power of beauty will sooner transform honesty from
what it is to a bawd than the force of honesty can
translate beauty into his likeness.

3.1.111–14

I hope your virtues will bring [me] to [my] wonted way
again.

3.1.40–41

We do sugar o'er the devil himself.

3.1.47–48

Take these again; for to the noble mind
Rich gifts wax poor when givers prove unkind.

3.1.100–101

If thou wilt needs marry, marry a fool; for wise men
know well enough what monsters you make of them.

3.1.139–41

You jig and amble, and you lisp, you nickname God's
    creatures, and make your wantonness your ignorance.
                                            3.1.146–48

In the very torrent, tempest and, . . . whirlwind of your
    passion, you must acquire and beget a temperance
    that may give it smoothness.
                                            3.2.5–8

I eat the air, promise-crammed.
                                            3.2.93–94

You are naught, you are naught.
                                            3.2.143

I distrust you.
                                            3.2.160

I do believe you think what now you speak.
                                            3.2.181

The lady doth protest too much, methinks.
                                            3.2.225

I could interpret between you and your love.
                                            3.2.241

Call me what instrument you will, though you fret me,
    you cannot play upon me.
                                            3.2.361–63

Heart with strings of steel,
Be soft as sinews of the new-born babe!
                                            3.3.70–71

This bodiless creation ecstasy
Is very cunning in.

3.4.140–41

Either [lodge] the devil or throw him out
With wondrous potency.

3.4.171–72

I must be cruel only to be kind.

3.4.180

There's matter in these sighs, these profound heaves,
You must translate. 'Tis fit we understand them.

4.1.1–2

I'll not be juggled with.

4.5.130

Are you like the painting of a sorrow,
A face without a heart?

4.7.107–8

I have a speech o' fire that fain would blaze
But that this folly douts it.

4.7.188–89

Where be your gibes now, your gambols, your songs,
    your flashes of merriment, that were wont to set the
    table on a roar?

5.1.183–85

[I] shall drink to [your] better breath.

5.2.268

LOVE'S LABOUR'S LOST

I think scorn to sigh: methinks I should outswear Cupid.
2.1.59–60

Your wit's too hot, it speeds too fast, 'twill tire.
2.1.119

Are you not the chief woman? you are the thickest here.
4.1.51–52

Look how you butt yourself in these sharp mocks.
5.2.251

Farewell, mad wench: you have a simple wit.
5.2.264

Twenty adieus, my frozen [Muscovite].
5.2.265

[Is this] the breed of wits so wonder'd at?
5.2.266

Nor God, nor I, delights in perjur'd men.
5.2.346

MEASURE FOR MEASURE

Thou art always figuring diseases in me; but thou art full
of error; I am sound.
1.2.48–49

One word, good friend . . . , a word with you.
A hundred—if they'll do you any good.
Is lechery so look'd after?
1.2.131–33

Thy head stands so tickle on thy shoulders, that a
   milkmaid, if she be in love, may sigh it off.
                                   1.2.161–63

        O fie, fie, fie!
What dost thou, or what art thou?
                                   2.2.172–73

That you might know [my pleasure] would much better
   please me,
Than to demand what 'tis.
                                   2.4.32–33

        But hear me;
Your sense pursues not mine: either you are ignorant,
Or seem so, crafty; and that's not good.
                                   2.4.73–75

If you be [a woman]—as you are well express'd
By all external warrants—show it now.
                                   2.4.135–36

I know your virtue hath a licence in't . . .
To pluck on others.
                                   2.4.144–46

[Your virtue] seems a little fouler than it is.
                                   2.4.145

        Thou are not certain;
For thy complexion shifts to strange effects
After the moon.
                                   3.1.23–25

O heavens, what stuff is here!
                                   3.2.5

I will pray . . . to increase your bondage.

3.2.71–72

Let me desire you to make your answer.

3.2.151–52

That fellow is a fellow of much license.

3.2.198

O, what may man within him hide,
Though angel on the outward side!

3.2.264–65

Do you persuade yourself that I respect you?

4.1.53

Come sir, leave me your snatches, and yield me a direct
answer.

4.2.5–6

Oftener ask forgiveness.

4.2.49

You are to do me both a present and a dangerous
courtesy.

4.2.160–61

Now is your time: speak loud, and kneel.

5.1.19–20

I hope you will not mock me with a husband.

5.1.415

THE MERRY WIVES OF WINDSOR

What, have I scaped love-letters in the holiday-time of
    my beauty, and am I now a subject for them? Let me
    see.
                                        2.1.1–3

How shall I be revenged on [you]? I think the best way
    were to entertain [you] with hope till the wicked fire
    of lust have melted [you] in [your] own grease.
                                        2.1.63–65

[You] woo both high and low, both rich and poor,
Both young and old, one with another,
[You] love the gallimaufry.
                                        2.1.110–12

A man may be too confident.
                                        2.1.178

I your lady? Alas, I should be a pitiful lady.
                                        3.3.46–47

Heaven make you better than your thoughts!
                                        3.3.190

O, what a world of vile ill-favour'd faults
Looks handsome in thee hundred pounds a year!
                                        3.4.32–33

Fate ordains [you] should be a cuckold.
                                        3.5.95–96

I'll provide you a chain, and I'll do what I can to get you
    a pair of horns.
                                        5.1.5–6

Better a little chiding than a great deal of heartbreak.
                                        5.3.9–10

Against such lewdsters and their lechery
Those that betray them do no treachery.
                                        5.3.21–22

Let there come a tempest of provocation, I will shelter
    me here.
                                        5.5.20–22

A MIDSUMMER NIGHT'S DREAM

What, [are you] jealous? . . .
I have forsworn [your] bed and company.
                                        2.1.61–62

These are the forgeries of jealousy.
                                        2.1.81

I love thee not, therefore pursue me not.
                                        2.1.188

Do I entice you? Do I speak you fair?
Or rather do I not in plainest truth
Tell you I do not, nor I cannot love you?
                                        2.1.199–201

But fare you well; perforce I must confess
I thought you lord of more true gentleness.
                                        2.2.130–31

O that a lady, of one man refus'd,
Should of another therefore be abus'd!
                                        2.2.132–33

Thou driv'st me past the bounds
Of maiden's patience.

                                        3.2.65–66

You do advance your cunning more and more
When truth kills truth, O devilish-holy fray!
                                        3.2.128

If you were men, as men you are in show,
You would not use a gentle lady so.
                                        3.2.151–52

The lunatic, the lover, and the poet
Are of imagination all compact:
One sees more devils than vast hell can hold.
                                        5.1.7–9

I kiss the wall's hole, not your lips at all.
                                        5.1.199

MUCH ADO ABOUT NOTHING

I wonder that you will still be talking . . . nobody marks
    you.
                                        1.1.107–8

What, my dear Lady Disdain! Are you yet living?
                                        1.1.109

I had rather hear my dog bark at a crow than a man
    swear he loves me.
                                        1.1.120–22

You always end with a jade's trick, I know you of old.
                                        1.1.133–34

OTHELLO

Be judge yourself
Whether I in any just term am affined
To love [you].

1.1.37–39

Have you lost your wits?

1.1.92

I have charged thee not to haunt about my doors.

1.1.95

In honest plainness thou hast heard me say
[I am] not for thee.

1.1.96–97

    O, [you] deceive
Past thought!

1.1.163–64

To mourn a mischief that is past and gone
Is the next way to draw new mischief on.

1.3.205–6

[How do I know but you are] no farther conscionable
    than in putting on the mere form of civil and humane
    seeming, for the better compassioning of [your] salt
    and most hidden loose affection?

2.1.236–39

[You are] handsome, young, and [hast] all those
    requisites . . . that folly and green minds look after.

2.1.243–45

Come, you are too severe a moraler.

2.3.294

I hope you will consider what is spoke
Comes from my love. But I do see you're moved.

                    3.3.220–21

Naked in bed, . . . and not mean harm?
It is hypocrisy against the devil!

                         4.1.5–6

[You are] persuaded I will marry [you], out of [your]
    own love and flattery, not out of my promise.

                    4.1.128–30

'Tis such another fitchew; marry, a perfumed one. What
    do you mean by this haunting of me?

                    4.1.145–46

        [Is] this the nature
Whom passion could not shake?

                         4.1.265–66

Dost thou in conscience think . . .
That there be women do abuse their husbands
In such gross kind?

                         4.3.60–62

Speak of me as I am.

                              5.2.340

PERICLES

'Tis time to fear when tyrants seem to kiss.

                              1.2.79

The cat, with eyne of burning coal,
Now couches 'fore the mouse's hole.

                              3.1.5–6

[Thou] dost with thine angel's face,
Seize with thine eagle's talons.

4.3.47–48

No visor does become black villainy
So well as soft and tender flattery.

4.4.44–45

ROMEO AND JULIET

You men, you beasts!

1.1.81

Here's much to do with hate, but more with love.

1.1.173

You burden love [with] too great oppression for a tender
thing.

1.4.23–24

Prick love for pricking and you beat love down.

1.4.28

In delay we waste our lights in vain.

1.4.44–45

Show a fair presence and put off these frowns,
An ill-beseeming semblance for a feast.

1.5.72–73

You kiss by th'book.

1.5.109

Be but sworn my love
And I'll no longer be a Capulet.

2.2.35–36

There lies more peril in thine eye
Than twenty . . . swords. Look thou but sweet
And I am proof against their enmity.

                         2.2.71–73

Dost thou love me? I know thou wilt say 'Ay',
And I will take thy word.

                         2.2.90–91

If thou swear'st [thou love me],
Thou mayst prove false. At lovers' perjuries,
They say, Jove laughs.

                         2.2.91–93

O swear not by the moon, th'inconstant moon,
That monthly changes in her circled orb,
Lest that thy love prove likewise variable.

                      2.2.109–11

What a change is here!
Is [she], that thou didst love so dear,
So soon forsaken?

                         2.3.61–63

     Young men's love then lies
Not truly in their hearts but in their eyes.

                         2.3.63–64

How much salt water thrown away in waste
To season love, that of it doth not taste.

                         2.3.67–68

     O, [I] know well
Thy love [doth] read by rote that [can] not spell.
                         2.3.83–84

Come young waverer, come, go with me.

2.3.85

These violent delights have violent ends
And in their triumph die, like fire and powder,
Which as they kiss consume.

2.6.9–11

Lovers can see to do their amorous rites
By their own beauties; or if love be blind,
It best agrees with night.

3.2.8–10

O serpent heart, hid with a flowering face.

3.2.73

Beautiful tyrant, fiend angelical,
Dove-feather'd raven, wolvish-ravening lamb!

3.2.75–76

Thou canst not speak of that thou dost not feel.

3.3.64

These times of woe afford no times to woo.

3.4.8

No man like [you] doth grieve my heart.

3.5.83

I will not marry yet. And when I do, I swear
It shall be [someone] whom you know I hate,
Rather than [you].

3.5.121–23

Romeo's a dishclout [compared to me].

3.5.219

Do not deny . . . that you love me.

4.1.24

O, bid me leap, rather than marry [someone else].

4.1.77

She's not well married that lives married young.

4.5.77

My heart itself plays 'My heart is full'.

4.5.104–5

THE TAMING OF THE SHREW

[You're] too rough for me.

1.1.55

From all such devils, good Lord deliver us!

1.1.66

That wench is stark mad or wonderful forward.

1.1.69

I am as peremptory as [you are] proud-minded;
And where two raging fires meet together,
They do consume the thing that feeds their fury.
Though little fire grows great with little wind,
Yet extreme guests will blow out fire and all.
So I to [you], and so [you] yield to me,
For I am rough and woo not like a babe.

2.1.131–37

You must not look so sour.

2.1.226

Now, for my life, the knave doth court my love.

3.1.47

In time I may believe, yet I mistrust.

3.1.49

Rescue thy mistress if thou be a man.

3.2.235

May you prove, sir, master of your art.

4.2.9

Kindness in women, not their beauteous looks,
Shall win my love.

4.2.41–42

THE TEMPEST

Let me remember thee what thou hast promis'd,
Which is not yet perform'd me.

1.2.243–44

[We] are both in either's pow'rs: but this swift business
I must uneasy make, less too light winning
Make the prize light.

1.2.453–55

If thou dost break [my] virgin-knot before
All sanctimonious ceremonies may
With full and holy rite be minister'd,
No sweet aspersion shall the heavens let fall
To make this contract grow.

4.1.15–19

Look thou be true.

4.1.51

Be more abstemious,
Or else, good night your vow!

4.1.53–54

I do forgive thee, unnatural though thou art.

5.1.78–79

Sweet lord, you play me false.

5.1.172

No, my dearest love,
I would not [play you false] for the world.

5.1.172–73

I'll be wise hereafter,
And seek for grace. What a thrice-double ass
Was I, to take this drunkard for a god,
And worship this dull fool!

5.1.294–97

Be free, and fare thou well!

5.1.317

TROILUS AND CRESSIDA

Though my heart's content firm love doth bear,
Nothing of that shall from mine eyes appear.

1.2.299–300

To make a sweet lady sad is a sour offence.

3.1.71

Is this the generation of love? Hot blood, hot thoughts,
and hot deeds? Why, they are vipers. Is love a
generation of vipers?

3.1.127–29

You have bereft me of all words, lady.

3.2.54

Words pay no debts, give [me] deeds.

3.2.55

They that have the voice of lions and the act of hares, are
they not monsters?

3.2.87–88

Perchance, my lord, I show more craft than love.

3.2.151

O heavens, you love me not!

4.4.81

[I am] as far high-soaring o'er thy praises
As thou unworthy to be call'd [my] servant.

4.4.122–23

The kiss you take is better than you give:
Therefore, no kiss.

4.5.38–39

Sweet honey Greek, tempt me no more to folly.

5.2.18

Good night; I'll be your fool no more.

5.2.32

Farewell! One eye yet looks on thee,
But with my heart the other eye doth see.
Ah, poor our sex! this fault in us I find:
The error of our eye directs our mind.

5.2.106–9

O, contain yourself:
Your passion draws ears hither.

5.2.179–80

TWELFTH NIGHT

How will [I] love, when the rich golden shaft
Hath kill'd the flock of all affections else
That live in [me].

1.1.30–37

What great ones do, the less with prattle of.

1.2.33

[You're] a great quarreller; and but that [you] hath the
    gift of a coward to allay the gust [you] hath in
    quarrelling, 'tis thought among the prudent [you]
    would quickly have the gift of a grave.

1.3.30–33

And you part so, mistress, I would I might never draw
    sword again. Fair lady, do you think you have fools in
    hand?

1.3.62–64

Many a good hanging prevents a bad marriage.

1.5.19

Excellently done, if God did it all.

1.5.239

I see you what you are, you are too proud:
But if you were the devil, you are fair.

1.5.254–55

How do [you] love me?

1.5.258

I cannot love [you]:
[You] might have took [your] answer long ago.

1.5.266–67

Not too fast: soft! soft!

1.5.297

Go shake your ears.

2.3.124

Marry sir, sometimes [you] are a kind of Puritan.

2.3.140

There is no woman's sides
Can bide the beating of so strong a passion
As love doth give my heart; no woman's heart
So big, to hold so much: [they] lack retention.

2.4.94–97

My love can give no place, bide no delay.

2.4.125

Here comes the little villain. How now, my metal of
    India?

2.5.13–14

Contemplation makes a rare turkey-cock of [you]: how
    [you] jet under [your] advanced plumes!

2.5.30–32

Wilt thou set thy foot o' my neck?

2.5.188

Now Jove, in his next commodity of hair, send thee a
    beard!
                                        3.1.45–46

Most excellent accomplished lady, the heavens rain
    odours on you!
                                        3.1.86–87

[I'll] force that on you in a shameful cunning
Which you knew none of yours.
                                        3.1.118–19

        O what a deal of scorn looks beautiful
In the contempt and anger of [your] lip!
A murd'rous guilt shows not itself more soon
Than love that would seem hid. Love's night is noon.
                                        3.1.147–50

[I] did show favour to the youth in your sight only to
    exasperate you, to awake your dormouse valour, to
    put fire in your heart, and brimstone in your liver.
                                        3.2.14–19

Draw, and as thou draw'st, swear horrible: for it comes
    to pass oft, that a terrible oath, with a swaggering
    accent sharply twanged off, gives manhood more
    approbation than ever proof itself would have earned
    him.
                                        3.4.179–83

I have said too much unto a heart of stone,
And laid mine honour too unchary out:
There's something in me that reproves my fault:
But such a headstrong potent fault it is,
That it but mocks reproof.
                                        3.4.205–7

Well, come again to-morrow. Fare thee well;
A fiend like thee might bear my soul to hell.
3.4.218–19

I hate ingratitude more in a man
Than lying, vainness, babbling drunkenness,
Or any taint of vice whose strong corruption
Inhabits our frail blood.
3.4.363–66

But O how vile an idol proves this god!
3.4.374

Madam, you have done me wrong,
Notorious wrong.
5.1.327–28

The Two Gentlemen of Verona

It boots thee not . . .
To be in love; where scorn is bought with groans;
Coy looks, with heart-sore sighs; one fading moment's
    mirth,
With twenty watchful, weary, tedious nights.
1.1.29–31

[Love is] but a folly bought with wit,
Or else a wit by folly vanquished.
1.1.34–35

Love is your master, for he masters you;
And he that is so yoked by a fool
Methinks should not be chronicled for wise.
1.1.39–41

As in the sweetest bud
The eating canker dwells, so eating Love
Inhabits in the finest wits of all.

1.1.42–44

Wherefore waste I time to counsel thee
That art a votary to fond desire?

1.1.51–52

[Your] little speaking shows [your] love but small.

1.2.29

Dare you presume to harbour wanton lines?
To whisper, and conspire against my youth?

1.2.42–43

Fie, fie; how wayward is this foolish love,
That (like a testy babe) will scratch the nurse,
And presently all humbled kiss the rod!

1.2.57–59

[You] make it strange, but [you] would be best pleas'd
To be so anger'd with another letter.

1.2.103–4

O, how this spring of love resembleth
The uncertain glory of an April day,
Which now shows all the beauty of the sun,
And by and by a cloud takes all away.

1.3.84–87

Not an eye that sees you but is a physician to comment
on your malady [of being in love].

2.1.39–40

Love is blind. O that you had mine eyes, or your own
   eyes had the lights they were wont to have.
                              2.1.67–68

Now, no discourse, except it be of love.
                              2.4.135

I will forget that [you are yet] alive,
Rememb'ring that my love to [you] is dead.
                              2.6.27–28

I do not seek to quench your love's hot fire,
But qualify the fire's extreme rage,
Lest it should burn above the bounds of reason.
                              2.7.21–23

The more thou damm'st [love] up, the more it burns:
The current that with gentle murmur glides,
Thou know'st, being stopp'd impatiently doth rage;
But when his fair course is not hindered,
He makes sweet music with th'enamell'd stones,
Giving a gentle kiss to every sedge
He overtaketh in his pilgrimage.
And so by many winding nooks he strays
With willing sport to the wild ocean.
                              2.7.24–32

That man that hath a tongue, I say is no man,
If with his tongue he cannot win a woman.
                              3.1.104–5

'Pox of your love-letters!
                              3.1.370–71

Think'st thou I am so shallow, so conceitless,
To be seduced by thy flattery,
That hast deceive'd so many with thy vows?

4.2.93–95

You dote on her that cares not for your love.

4.4.82

Love will not be spurr'd to what it loathes.

5.2.7

Be gone, solicit me no more.

5.4.40

If the gentle spirit of moving words
Can no way change you to a milder form,
I'll woo you like a soldier, at arm's end,
And love you 'gainst the nature of love: force ye.

5.4.55–58

    O heaven, were man
But constant, he were perfect. That one error
Fills him with faults; makes him run through all th' sins.

5.4.109–11

THE WINTER'S TALE

[You] shall not stay,
[I'll] thwack [you] hence with distaffs.

1.2.36–37

You put me off with limber vows.

1.2.47

Will you go yet?
Force me to keep you as a prisoner,
Not like a guest?

1.2.51–53

O, that is entertainment
My bosom likes not, nor my brows.

1.2.118–19

Go, play, boy, play.

1.2.187

Let's have that, good sir.
Come on, sit down, come on, and do your best
To fright me with your sprites: you're powerful at it.

2.1.26–28

Not so hot, good sir.

2.3.32

Sir: my gracious lord,
To chide at your extremes, it not becomes me.

4.4.5–6

Your eye hath too much youth in 't.

5.1.224

Propositioning

Sex is always in the wings in Shakespeare. But then again there's all that foreplay and fiddling about in front of the gods and everyone. Come to think of it, every other word has a double meaning. Shakespeare's curtains are always going up on sex.

Drift off to sleep in any performance and wake with a start: they'll be talking sex or something that sounds a lot like it. Shakespeare is laced with innuendo. Or unlaced. Here's excuse to be risqué. If he can come across all firm and earthy, so can you. If he can suggest entanglements in cultivated tones, you can, too.

Everyone wants to feel desirable, including the one you desire. Do them the grace of satisfaction. The response you want already exists in them, just waiting for opportunity. Their eagerness and yours need only meet. Invite them to their own party.

People often flop at propositioning because they've never learned not to be blatant. They get no response because no one likes to be thought of as cheap. What are needed are reasons to yield, or at least good excuses. What unleashes true passion is rationalization. Something in the ear, just a fragment of thought, a little lagniappe in the line of language. There may be no reality beyond the moment, but at least care enough to create illusions.

Shakespeare's arousing phrases are exactly what you need when you get to the major point of seduction. In fact, Shakespeare gets right to the point, wishing happiness to the sheets, fragrances to heaven. Pleasure's art is at your fingertip as you peruse these prurient lines. Strip away neglect, slip off the constraints of shyness. Finally find a good use for literature.

ALL'S WELL THAT ENDS WELL

It is not politic in the commonwealth of nature to
    preserve virginity.

                              1.1.125–26

Loss of virginity is rational increase, and there was never
    virgin got till virginity was first lost.

                              1.1.126–27

Virginity breeds mites, much like a cheese; consumes
    itself to the very paring, and so dies with feeding his
    own stomach.

                              1.1.139–41

[Virginity is] a commodity will lose the gloss with lying;
    the longer kept, the less worth. Off with't while 'tis
    vendible; answer the time of request.

                              1.1.149–51

    Tis pity . . .
That wishing well had not a body in't
Which might be felt.

                              1.1.175–78

My poor body, madam, requires it; I am driven on by the
    flesh, and he must needs go that the devil drives.

                              1.3.26–28

I have been, madam, a wicked creature, as you and all
    flesh and blood are, and indeed I do marry that I may
    repeat.

                              1.3.33–35

You have restrain'd yourself within the list of too cold an
    adieu.

                              2.1.50–51

How, Dian, from thy altar do I fly,
And to imperial Love, that god most high
Do my sighs stream.

2.3.74–76

Be not afraid that I your hand should take;
I'll never do you wrong, for your own sake.
Blessing upon your vows, and in your bed
Find fairer fortune if you ever wed!

2.3.89–92

If the quick fire of youth light not your mind
You are no maiden but a monument.

4.2.5–6

When you are dead you should be such a one
As you are now; for you are cold and stern,
And now you should be as your mother was
When your sweet self was got.

4.2.7–10

Stand no more off,
But give thyself unto my sick desires,
Who then recovers.

4.2.34–36

I like [you]
And [I'll] board [you] i' th' wanton way of youth.

5.3.209–10

ANTONY AND CLEOPATRA

Come, my queen!
Last night you did desire it.

1.1.55–56

You think none but your sheets are privy to your wishes.
                            1.2.43–44

        I can do nothing
But what indeed is honest to be done.
Yet have I fierce affections, and think
What Venus did with Mars.

                            1.5.16–19

        Give me a kiss.
Even this repays me.

                            3.11.70–71

        Come,
Let's have one other gaudy night.

                            3.13.187–88

        Come on, my queen,
There's sap in't yet!

                            3.13.196–97

        Spend that kiss
Which is my heaven to have.

                            5.2.301–2

As You Like It

Unless you teach me to forget, . . . you must not learn
    me how to remember any extraordinary pleasure.
                            1.2.3–6

Come, come, wrestle with thy affections.
                            1.3.20

Go with me to [my place], and I'll show it you.
                            3.2.418

O come, let us remove.

3.4.52

Take [me] to thee.

3.5.64

I would kiss before I spoke.

4.1.69

Will you persever to enjoy [me]?

5.2.4

Consent . . . that we may enjoy each other.

5.2.9

You have my consent. Let [the] wedding be tomorrow.

5.2.13–14

[We] have made a pair of stairs to marriage, which [we]
    will climb incontinent, or else be incontinent before
    marriage.

5.2.36–38

I do desire it with all my heart; and I hope it is no
    dishonest desire, to desire to be a woman of the
    world.

5.3.3–5

[I would have you] should I die the hour after.

5.4.12

I desire you [and] I press in here . . . amongst the rest of
    the country copulatives, to swear and forswear,
    according as marriage binds and blood breaks.

5.4.54–57

We will begin these rites,
As we do trust they'll end, in true delights.
                                    5.4.196–97

CYMBELINE

[I wish] I had this cheek
To bathe my lips upon.
                                    1.7.99–100

Let me my service tender on your lips.
                                    1.7.140

How bravely thou becom'st thy bed! fresh lily!
                                    2.2.15

That I might touch!
But kiss, one kiss.
                                    2.2.16–17

If [I] can penetrate [you] with [my] fingering, so: we'll
    try with tongue too.
                                    2.3.13–14

I'll make a journey twice as far, t'enjoy
A second night of such sweet shortness which
Was mine in Britain.
                                    2.4.43–45

[Your] pretty action did outsell [your] gift,
And yet enrich'd it too.
                                    2.4.102–3

        Under [your] breast
(Worthy [your] pressing) lies a mole, right proud
Of that most delicate lodging. By my life,

[If] I kiss'd it, [would] give me present hunger
To feed again, though full.

2.4.134–38

How hard it is to hide the sparks of Nature!

3.3.79

HAMLET

Like a puff'd and reckless libertine [yourself] the
primrose path of dalliance treads.

1.3.49–50

When the blood burns, how prodigal the soul
Lends the tongue vows.

1.3.116–17

In [me] . . . [desire] too much o'er leavens
The form of plausive manners.

1.4.23–30

Lewdness courts [me] in a shape of heaven.

1.5.54

Lust, though to a radiant angel link'd,
Will sate itself in a celestial bed.

1.5.55–56

Swift as quicksilver [I will] course through
The natural gates and alleys of [your] body.

1.5.66–67

[I am] open to incontinency.

2.1.30

[Take me] by the wrist and hold me hard.

2.1.87

I much did long to see you,
The need I have to use you did provoke
[My] hasty sending.

2.2.1–4

Being of so young days . . .
Draw [me] on to pleasures.

2.2.11–15

Heavens make [my] presence and our practices
Pleasant [to you].

2.2.38–39

[Your] impotence was falsely borne in hand.

2.2.66–67

[I long to be in your] excellent white bosom.

2.2.112

[I could] live about [your] waist, or in the middle of
    [your] favours.

2.2.232–33

There is a kind of confession in your looks, which your
    modesties have not craft enough to colour.

2.2.279–80

The lover shall not sigh gratis.

2.2.320–21

We'll e'en to't like French falconers, fly at anything we
    see.

2.2.425–26

[Let's] run barefoot up and down.

2.2.501

Drive [my] purpose into these delights.

3.1.27

Wouldst thou be a breeder of sinners?

3.1.121–22

[I] suck'd the honey of [your] music vows.

3.1.158

Be not too tame.

3.2.16

Lady, shall I lie in your lap?

3.2.110–11

That's a fair thought to lie between maids' legs.

3.2.117

[Let's] make passionate action.

3.2.133 Stage Direction

Love our hearts and Hymen . . . our hands
Unite commutual in most sacred bands.

3.2.154–55

You are keen, my lord, you are keen.

3.2.243

It would cost you a groaning to take off my edge.

3.2.244

To flaming youth let virtue be as wax
And melt in her own fire.

3.4.84–85

Proclaim no shame
When the compulsive ardour gives the charge.
3.4.85–86

        [Let us] live
In the rank sweat of an enseamed bed,
. . . honeying and making love.
3.4.91–93

My pulse as yours doth temperately keep time,
And makes as healthful music.
3.4.142–43

Let [me] tempt you again to bed.
3.4.184

[I would] pinch wanton on your cheek.
3.4.185

[You rouse] excitements of my reason and my blood.
4.4.58

Our indiscretion sometime serves us well.
5.2.8

Come, and take this hand from me.
5.2.221

LOVE'S LABOUR'S LOST

Price you yourselves: what buys your company?
5.2.224

MEASURE FOR MEASURE

Let us withdraw together,
And we may soon our satisfaction have.

                    1.1.81–82

Upon a true contract I got possession of [your] bed.

                    1.2.134–35

Quite athwart goes all decorum.

                    1.3.30–31

Feel the wanton stings and motions of the sense.

                    1.4.58–59

I shall follow [you] as the flesh and fortune shall better
     determine.

                    2.1.250–51

Kneel down before [me], hang upon [my] gown;
You are too cold.

                    2.2.44–45

Ay, touch [me]: there's the vein.

                    2.2.70

I am that way going to temptation.

                    2.2.159

Dost thou desire [me] foully for those things
That make [me] good?

                    2.2.174–75

          Most dangerous
Is that temptation that doth goad us on
To sin in loving virtue.

                    2.2.181–83

In my heart the strong and swelling evil
Of my conception [lusts for you].

2.4.6–7

I desire access to you.

2.4.18

'Tis [forbidden] in heaven, but not in earth.

2.4.50

Give up your body to . . . sweet uncleanness.

2.4.54

I had rather give my body than my soul.

2.4.56

Might there not be a charity in sin?

2.4.63

I'll take it as a peril to my soul;
It is no sin at all, but charity.

2.4.65–66

You must lay down the treasures of your body.

2.4.96

[Come to] a bed
That longing have been sick for.

2.4.102–3

[This is more] a merriment than a vice.

2.4.116

From this testimony of your own sex . . . let me be bold.

2.4.130–32

I have no tongue but one; gentle my lord.

2.4.138

Give me love.

2.4.143

I have begun,
And now I give my sensual race the rein.

2.4.158–59

Fit thy consent to my sharp appetite.

2.4.160

Lay by all nicety and prolixious blushes
That banish what they sue for.

2.4.161–62

Yield up thy body to my will.

2.4.163

Hook both right and wrong to th'appetite,
To follow as it draws!

2.4.175–76

[I could] bark your honour from that trunk you bear,
And leave you naked.

3.1.71–72

Dost thou think . . .
If I would yield [you] my virginity
Thou mightst be freed?

3.1.96–98

This night's the time
That I should do what I abhor to name.

3.1.100–1

Sure, it is no sin;
Or of the deadly seven it is the least.

> 3.1.109–10

[I'll give you] sensible warm motion . . . and [a]
delighted spirit.

> 3.1.119–20

Let me live.
What sin you do to save [my] life,
Nature dispenses with the deed so far
That it becomes a virtue.

> 3.1.132–35

If for this night [I] entreat you to [my] bed, give [me]
promise of satisfaction.

> 3.1.263–64

Fie, sirrah, a bawd, a wicked bawd.

> 3.2.18

[I am] ever your fresh whore.

> 3.2.57

A little more lenity to lechery would do no harm in
[you].

> 3.2.94–95

[Come with me] this downright way of creation.

> 3.2.101

For the rebellion of a codpiece!

> 3.2.110–11

[I'd like to] fill a bottle with a tun-dish.

> 3.2.166

Good my lord, be good to me.

3.2.185

It is not my consent, but my entreaty too.

4.1.67–68

The best and wholesom'st spirits of the night
Envelop you!

4.2.71–72

If bawdy talk offend you, we'll have very little of it.

4.3.175–176

[I offer the] gift of my chaste body
To [your] concupiscible intemperate lust.

5.1.100–101

I will go darkly to work with [you].

5.1.277

That's the way; for women are light at midnight.

5.1.278

THE MERRY WIVES OF WINDSOR

I spy entertainment in [you]: [you] discourse, [you]
    carve, [you] give the leer of invitation; I can construe
    the action of [your] familiar style.

1.3.41–43

Even now [you] gave me good eyes too, examined my
    parts with most judicious oeillades: sometimes the
    beam of [your] view gilded my foot, sometimes my
    portly belly.

1.3.55–58

O, [you] did so course o'er my exteriors with such a
greedy intention that the appetite of [your] eye did
seem to scorch me up like a burning-glass!
1.3.61–63

[I'll] lead [you] on with a fine-baited delay till [you]
have pawned [your] horses.
2.1.92–93

I pray . . . come a little nearer this ways.
2.2.45–46

I'll make more of thy old body than I have done . . .
Good body, I thank thee. Let them say 'tis grossly
done; so it be fairly done, no matter.
2.2.133–38

[You] give me the potions and the motions.
3.1.94–95

If [I] take [you], let [me] take [you] simply.
3.2.69–70

I love thee; help me away. Let me creep in here.
3.3.130

What would you with me?
3.4.59

[My] husband goes this morning a-birding; [I] desire
you once more to come to [me], between eight and
nine.
3.5.40–42

[Let us] embrace, kiss, protest, and, as it were, speak the
prologue of our comedy.
3.5.67–68

Come up into my chamber.

4.5.122

Heaven prosper our sport!

5.2.12

Now, the hot-blooded gods assist me!

5.5.2

Remember, Jove, thou wast a bull for thy Europa.

5.5.3

O powerful love, that in some respects makes a beast a
man; in some other, a man a beast.

5.5.4–6

When gods have hot backs, what shall poor men do?

5.5.11–12

Send me a cool rut-time, Jove.

5.5.13–14

Raise up the organs of [your] fantasy.

5.5.52

A MIDSUMMER NIGHT'S DREAM

I will aggravate my voice so, that I will roar you as gently
as any sucking dove; I will roar you and 'twere any
nightingale.

1.2.76–78

I might see young Cupid's fiery shaft
Quench'd in the chaste beams of the watery moon.

2.1.161–62

The moon, methinks, looks with a watery eye,
And when she weeps, weeps every little flower,
Lamenting some enforced chastity.
Tie up my love's tongue, bring him silently.

3.1.191–94

Sleep thou, and I will wind thee in my arms.

4.1.39

Come my queen, take hands with me,
And rock the ground whereon these sleepers be.

4.1.84–85

O kiss me through the hole of this vile wall.

5.1.198

OTHELLO

[Let us make] the beast with two backs.

1.1.115

You have been hotly called for.

1.2.44

These arms of mine . . . have used their dearest action.

1.3.84–86

I do confess the vices of my blood.

1.3.125

Come . . . I have but an hour
Of love, of worldly matter and direction
To spend with thee. We must obey the time.

1.3.299–301

Our bodies are gardens, to the which our wills are
gardeners.

1.3.321–22

[Let us] cool our raging motions, our carnal stings, our
unbitted lusts.

1.3.331–32

If thou canst cuckold him, thou dost thyself a pleasure,
me a sport.

1.3.369–70

Make love's quick pants in [my] arms.

2.1.80

You rise to play, and go to bed to work.

2.1.115

[May kisses] the greatest discords be
That o'er our hearts shall make.

2.1.196–97

Lay thy finger thus, and let thy soul be instructed.

2.1.219

[Your] eye must be fed, and what delight shall [you]
have!

2.1.223–24

[My courtesy is] an index and obscure prologue to the
history of lust and foul thoughts.

2.1.255–56

[We meet] so near with [our] lips that [our] breaths
embrace together. . . . When these mutualities so

marshal the way, hard at hand comes the master and
main exercise, th'incorporate conclusion.

2.1.257–61

Have a shorter journey to your desires.

2.1.275–76

Come my dear love,
The purchase made, the fruits are to ensue:
That profit's yet to come 'tween me and you.

2.3.7–10

[I have] not yet made wanton the night with [you], and
[you are] sport for Jove.

2.3.16–17

I'll warrant [you are] full of game.

2.3.19

Well: happiness to [our] sheets!

2.3.26

Pleasure and action make the hours seem short.

2.3.374

[I want to] taste [your] sweet body.

3.3.349

I see, sir, you are eaten up with passion.

3.3.394

You would be satisfied?

3.3.396

> Wring my hand,
> Cry 'O sweet creature!' and then kiss me hard
> As if [you] plucked up kisses by the roots.
>
> 3.3.423–25

> Lay [thy] leg o'er my thigh,
> And sigh, and kiss, and then cry 'Cursed fate'!
>
> 3.3.426–27

> All my fond love thus do I blow to heaven.
>
> 3.3.448

> Give me your hand. This hand is moist, my lady . . .
> This argues fruitfulness and liberal heart:
> Hot, hot, and moist.
>
> 3.4.36–39

> [You are] amiable and subdue [me]
> Entirely to [your] love.
>
> 3.4.61–62

> Thither comes the bauble.
>
> 4.1.134

> Fall me thus about my neck!
>
> 4.1.135

> Hang and loll and weep upon me, so shake and pull me!
>
> 4.1.138–39

> [I'll] pluck [you] to my chamber.
>
> 4.1.140–41

> I kiss the instrument of [your] pleasures.
>
> 4.1.218

Lay on my bed my wedding sheets.

4.2.107

You shall be satisfied.

4.2.246

Kill me tomorrow, let me live tonight!

5.2.79

PERICLES

The beauty of this sinful dame
Made many princes thither frame,
To seek her as a bed-fellow,
In marriage-pleasures play-fellow.

1.Chorus.31–34

[You come in] clothed like a bridge,
For the embracements even of Jove himself.

1.1.7–8

[Your] golden fruit [is] dangerous to be touch'd.

1.1.29

[I'm made] advent'rous by desire.

1.1.36

You are a fair viol, and your sense the strings,
Who, finger'd to make man his lawful music,
Would draw heaven down and all the gods to hearken.

1.1.82–84

Let none disturb us.

1.2.1

Pleasure's art can joy my spirits.

1.2.10

That were to blow at fire in hope to quench it.

1.4.4

Why sir, say if you [make love to me], who takes offence
At that would make me glad?

2.5.70–71

Nay, come, your hands and lips must seal it too.

2.5.84

It pleaseth me so well, that I will see you wed;
And then, with what haste you can, get you to bed.

2.5.91–92

Come, give me your flowers.

4.1.26

Let's have fresh [wenches], what'er we pay for them.

4.2.10–11

Performance shall follow.

4.2.59

You are light into my hands, where you are like to live.

4.2.68

If it please the gods to defend you by men, then men
   must comfort you, men must feed you, men stir
   you up.

4.2.87–88

These blushes of [yours] must be quench'd with some
   present practice.

4.2.122–24

Giving out [your] beauty stirs up the lewdly inclin'd.
4.2.141–42

[Will you] do the deeds of darkness?
4.6.28

Pray you, without any more virginal fencing, will you use
[me] kindly? [I] will line your apron with gold.
4.6.56–58

Now, pretty one, how long have you been at this trade?
4.6.65–66

Come, bring me to some private place; come come.
4.6.89–90

Will you not go the way of women-kind?
4.6.149–50

O, come hither.
5.1.194

I am wild in my beholding.
O heavens bless my girl.
5.1.221–22

On the touching of [your] lips I may melt.
5.3.42–43

O come, be buried . . . within these arms.
5.3.43–44

Draw thy tool.

1.1.30

My naked weapon is out.

1.1.32

Then [have you] sworn that [you] will still live chaste?
[If so, you] in that sparing make huge waste.

1.1.215–16

Beauty starv'd with [your] severity
Cuts beauty off from all posterity.

1.1.217–18

Such comfort as do lusty young men feel
When well-apparell'd April on the heel
Of limping winter treads, even such delight
Among fresh female buds shall you this night
Inherit at my house.

1.2.26–30

Go, girl, seek happy nights to happy days.

1.3.105

If love be rough with you, be rough with love.

1.4.27

Let wantons light of heart
Tickle the senseless rushes with their heels.

1.4.35–36

On, lusty gentlemen.

1.4.113

Quench the fire, the room is grown too hot.

1.5.28

This unlook'd-for sport comes well.

1.5.29

Touching [yours], [I'll] make blessed my rude hand.

1.5.50

Good pilgrim, you do wrong your hand too much,
Which mannerly devotion shows in this;
For saints have hands that pilgrims' hands do touch,
And palm to palm is holy palmers' kiss.

1.5.96–99

Let lips do what hands do.

1.5.102

Move not, while my prayer's effect I take.
Thus from my lips, by thine, my sin is purg'd.

1.5.105–6

Sin from my lips? O trespass sweetly urg'd.
Give me my sin again.

1.5.108–9

Blind is his love, and best befits the dark.

2.1.32

If love be blind, love cannot hit the mark.

2.1.33

    Pardon me,
And not impute this yielding to light love
Which the dark night hath so discovered.

2.2.104–6

O wilt thou leave me so unsatisfied?
2.2.125

I should kill thee with much cherishing.
2.2.183

For this drivelling love is like a great natural that runs
lolling up and down to hide his bauble in a hole.
2.4.91–93

The bawdy hand of the dial is now upon the prick of
noon.
2.4.111–12

Had [you] affections and warm youthful blood
[You] would be as swift in motion as a ball.
2.5.12–13

O God's lady dear,
Are you so hot?
2.5.62–63

Now comes the wanton blood up in your cheeks.
They'll be in scarlet straight.
2.5.71–72

[My] love
Must climb a bird's nest soon when it is dark.
2.5.74–75

So smile the heavens upon this holy act
That after-hours with sorrow chide us not.
2.6.1–2

Come, come with me and we will make short work,
For . . . you shall not stay alone.

2.6.35–36

Men's eyes were made to look, and let them gaze.

3.1.53

Spread thy close curtain, love-performing night,
That [my lover may]
Leap to these arms untalk'd-of and unseen.

3.2.5–7

[Let us] think true love acted [is only] simple modesty.

3.2.16

Give me my [lover].

3.2.20–21

O, I have bought the mansion of a love
But not possess'd it.

3.2.26–27

Though I am sold,
[I am] not yet enjoy'd.

3.2.27–28

[I desire to] seize
On the white wonder of [your] dear hand
And steal immortal blessing from [your] lips.

3.3.35–37

[Your lips] even in pure and vestal modesty
Still blush, as thinking their own kisses sin.

3.3.38–39

Rouse thee, man. Thy [lover] is alive.

3.3.134

O how my heart abhors
To hear [you] nam'd, and cannot come to [you]
To wreak . . . love . . .
Upon [your] body.

3.5.99–102

Mistress minion you,
Thank me no thankings nor proud me no prouds,
But fettle your fine joints.

3.5.151–53

Sleep for a week; for the next night . . . you shall rest but
little!

4.5.5–7

I dreamt [you] came . . .
And breath'd such life with kisses in my lips
That I reviv'd and was an emperor.

5.1.6–9

I will lie with thee tonight.

5.1.34

Tempt not a desperate man.

5.3.59

I will kiss thy lips.

5.3.164

Thy lips are warm!

5.3.167

THE TAMING OF THE SHREW

Madam, undress you and come now to bed.
Induction.2.118

Come, madam wife, sit by my side
And let the world slip, we shall ne'er be younger.
Induction.2.141–42

I will board [you] though [you] chide as loud
As thunder when the clouds in autumn crack.
1.2.94–95

Now, by the world, it is a lusty wench.
2.1.160

Come, sit on me.
2.1.198

Women are made to bear, and so are you.
2.1.200

Did ever Dian so become a grove
As Kate this chamber with her princely gait?
O be thou Dian, and let her be Kate,
And then let Kate be chaste and Dian sportful.
2.1.252–55

Come . . . we'll to bed.
5.2.185

THE TEMPEST

Lend thy hand, and pluck my magic garment from me.

1.2.23–24

Lie there my Art.

1.2.24

I come to answer thy best pleasure.

1.2.189–90

Go make thyself a nymph o' th' sea.

1.2.301

I prithee now, lead the way, without any more talking.

2.2.173–74

[I] dare not offer
What I desire to give; and much less take
What I shall die to want.

3.1.77–79

Hymen's lamps shall light you.

4.1.23

Do not give dalliance
Too much the rein: the strongest oaths are straw
To th' fire in' th' blood.

4.1.51–53

Cold nymphs [wear] chaste crowns.

4.1.66

[Come] contract of true love to celebrate.

4.1.84

Mars's hot minion is return'd again.

4.1.98

Where the bee sucks, there suck I.

5.1.88

For more assurance that a living Prince
Does now speak to thee, I embrace thy body.

5.1.108–9

Troilus and Cressida

[You are] stubborn-chaste against all suit.

1.1.97

I would my heart were in [your] body.

1.2.78–79

You have the honey.

2.2.145

What says my sweet queen, my very very sweet queen?

3.1.78–79

[I] eat nothing but doves, love, and that breeds hot
blood, and hot blood begets hot thoughts, and hot
thoughts beget hot deeds, and hot deeds is love.

3.1.123–26

Honey-sweet queen!

3.1.137

Give me swift transportance to those fields
Where I may wallow in the lily beds.

3.2.10–11

I am giddy: expectation whirls me round.
Th'imaginary relish is so sweet
That it enchants my sense: what will it be
When that the wat'ry palate tastes indeed
Love's thrice-repured nectar.

3.2.16–20

I fear me . . . some joy too fine . . .
For the capacity of my ruder powers.

3.2.20–23

Such a passion doth embrace my bosom.

3.2.34

I do beseech you pardon me:
'Twas not my purpose thus to beg a kiss.
I am asham'd. O heavens, what have I done?

3.2.135–37

I will show you a chamber with bed, which bed, because
    it shall not speak of your pretty encounters, press it
    to death!

3.2.206–8

I prithee now, to bed.

4.2.7

Night hath been too brief.

4.2.11

Would [you] not—ah, naughty man—let it sleep?
4.2.32–33

We two, that with so many thousand sighs
Did buy each other, must poorly sell ourselves
With the rude brevity and discharge of one.

4.4.38–40

The lustre in your eye, heaven in your cheek,
Pleads your fair usage.

                                        4.4.116–17

I'll have my kiss . . . Lady, by your leave.

                                        4.5.35

In kissing, do you render or receive?

                                        4.5.36

May I, sweet lady, beg a kiss of you?

                                        4.5.47

For Venus' sake, give me a kiss.

                                        4.5.49

        Fie, fie upon [you]!
There's language in [your] eye, [your] cheek, [your]
    lip—
Nay, [your] foot speaks; [your] wanton spirits look out
At every joint and motive of [your] body.

                                        4.5.54–57

O, these encounterers, so glib of tongue,
That give accosting welcome ere it comes,
And wide unclasp the tables of their thoughts
To every ticklish reader: set them down
For sluttish spoils of opportunity
And daughters of the game.

                                        4.5.58–63

I'll take that winter from your lips, fair lady.

                                        4.5.124

[I] will sing any man at first sight.

                                        5.2.9

Any man may sing [me], if he can take [my] clef: [I'm]
noted.

5.2.10–11

TWELFTH NIGHT

Now, sir, thought is free. I pray you bring your hand to
th' buttery bar and let it drink.

1.3.68–69

It is legs and thighs. Let me see thee caper. Ha, higher!
1.3.138–39

You do usurp yourself: for what is yours to bestow is not
yours to reserve.

1.5.188–90

Lady, you are the cruell'st she alive
If you will lead these graces to the grave
And leave the world no copy.

1.5.244–46

They that dally nicely with words may quickly make
them wanton.

3.1.14–15

My matter hath no voice, lady, but to your own most
pregnant and vouchsafed ear.

3.1.90–91

Give me your hand sir.

3.1.96

Wilt thou go to bed?

3.4.30

To bed? Ay, sweetheart, and I'll come to thee.

3.4.31

Will you deny me now?
Is't possible that my deserts to you
Can lack persuasion? Do not tempt my misery,
Lest that it make me so unsound a man
As to upbraid you with those kindnesses
That I have done for you.

3.4.356–61

THE TWO GENTLEMEN OF VERONA

They do not love that do not show their love.

1.2.31

My bosom, as a bed,
Shall lodge thee till thy wound be thoroughly heal'd.

1.2.115–16

I search it with a sovereign kiss.

1.2.117

Seal the bargain with a holy kiss.

2.2.7

Upon a homely object, Love can wink.

2.4.93

Now can I break my fast, dine, sup, and sleep
Upon the very naked name of Love.

2.4.136–37

When it stands well with him, it stands well with her.
2.5.20–21

[You've] become a notable lover.
2.5.37

[You've] become a hot lover.
2.5.43

Didst thou but know the inly touch of love,
Thou wouldst as soon go kindle fire with snow
As seek to quench the fire of love with words.
2.7.18–20

I'll be as patient as a gentle stream,
And make a pastime of each weary step,
Till the last step have brought me to my love,
And there I'll rest, as after much turmoil
A blessed soul doth in Elysium.
2.7.34–38

Thou shalt be worshipp'd, kiss'd, lov'd, and ador'd.
4.4.197

THE WINTER'S TALE

We will give you sleepy drinks, that your senses
(unintelligent of our insufficience) may, though they
cannot praise us, as little accuse us.
1.1.13–16

There rooted betwixt [us] then such an affection which
cannot choose but branch now.
1.1.23–24

You may ride's
With one soft kiss a thousand furlongs ere
With spur we heat an acre.

1.2.94–96

How now, you wanton calf!
Art thou my calf?

1.2.126–27

Is whispering nothing?
Is leaning cheek to cheek? is meeting noses?
Kissing with inside lip? stopping the career
Of laughter with a sigh? . . .
. . . horsing foot on foot?
Skulking in corners? wishing clocks more swift?
Hours, minutes? noon, midnight? and all eyes
Blind . . . but [ours]; [ours] only.

1.2.284–91

You'll kiss me hard, and speak to me as if I were a baby
still.

2.1.5–6

You'd wanton with us,
If we would have you.

2.1.18–19

She was a woman, and was turned into a cold fish for she
would not exchange flesh with one that loved her.

4.4.280–82

I might have look'd upon my queen's full eyes,
Have taken treasure from her lips, and left them
More rich for what they yielded.

5.1.53–55

Let no man mock me,
For I will kiss [you].

5.3.79–80

O, [you're] warm!
If this be magic, let it be an art
Lawful as eating.

5.3.109–11

Propositioning | 231

Whining and
Wheedling

IF YOUR CHARM gets you only so far, you may need something even more underhanded to break down your quarry's trenchant resistance to your seduction. Try guilt. Shakespeare borrowed this powerful instrument for tough cases. Where'd he get it? From the weak. He transformed and twisted it into his own words, and it came out as whining and wheedling. Shakespeare wielded the power of well-placed and well-timed emotional pressure. Learn from the master of manipulation.

Far too many people have a deep compulsion to be nice. Or rather to be seen as nice. They cry out for provocation. Guilt is the answer. Give your desired a chance to show off their wonderfulness by being wonderful to you. Provide nice boys and good girls with the affirmation they crave. They love to atone.

Whining is high-pitched complaining; wheedling is flattery leveraged with expectation. This is sophisticated strategy that works only if your feelings are the feelings your quarry cares about. You can whine and wheedle with abandon, but only after that person has a strong attachment to you. Once you've hooked them, wear them down. But which tactic do you use? Either, neither, both?

Your whining tells someone they're bad—so they'll do all they can to be good again. Call your love a hard-hearted adamant. Or an uncivil lady. Wheedling tells them how vital to your existence they are—so they'll do all they can to live up to your dreams. "There's no one living but you. Show pity or I die!"

All's Well That Ends Well

My imagination
Carries no favour in't but [yours].

1.1.80–81

There is no living, none,
If [you] be away.

1.1.82–83

I know I love in vain, strive against hope;
Yet in this captious and inteemable sieve
I still pour in the waters of my love
And lack not to lose still.

1.3.196–99

O then, give pity
To her whose state is such that cannot choose
But lend and give where she is sure to lose.

1.3.208–10

[O pity her]
That seeks not to find that her search implies,
But riddle-like lives sweetly where she dies!

1.3.211–12

Thy will by my performance shall be serv'd.

2.1.201

Sir, I am a poor friend of yours that loves you.

2.2.42

I dare not say I take you, but I give
Me and my service, ever whilst I live,
Into your guiding power.

2.3.102–4

Sir, I can nothing say
But that I am your most obedient servant . . .
And ever shall
With true observance seek to eke out that
wherein toward me my homely stars have fail'd
To equal my great fortune.

2.5.75

What angel shall
Bless this unworthy husband?

3.4.25–26

I love thee
By love's own sweet constraint, and will for ever
Do thee all rights of service.

4.2.15–17

Say thou art mine, and ever
My love as it begins shall so persever.

4.2.36–37

Here, take my ring;
My house, mine honour, yea, my life be thine,
And I'll be bid by thee.

4.2.51–53

[Your] dear perfection hearts that scorn'd to serve
Humbly call'd mistress.

5.3.18–19

[You] knew [your] distance and did angle for me,
Madding my eagerness with [your] restraint,
As all impediments in fancy's course
Are motives of more fancy; and in fine
[Your] inf'nite cunning with [your] modern grace
Subdu'd me to [your] rate.

5.3.211–16

What should I do, I do not?

1.3.9

The strong necessity of time commands
Our services awhile, but my full heart
Remains in use with you.

1.3.43–45

    May I never,
To this good purpose that so fairly shows,
Dream of impediment!

2.2.152–54

    Thou knewst too well
My heart was to thy rudder tied by th' strings
And thou shouldst tow me after.

3.11.56–58

    O'er my spirit
Thy full supremacy thou knewst, and that
Thy beck might from the bidding of the gods
Command me.

3.11.58–61

    You did know
How much you were my conqueror, and that
My sword, made weak by my affection, would
Obey it on all cause.

3.11.65–68

    [I do] confess thy greatness,
Submits [me] to thy might.

3.12.16–17

I kiss [your] conqu'ring hand.

                                        3.13.79

          Whate'er becomes of me,
This is a soldier's kiss. Rebukable
And worthy shameful check it were, to stand
On more mechanic compliment.

                                        4.5.29–32

          O thou day o'th' world,
Chain mine armed neck! Leap thou, attire and all,
Through proof of harness to my heart, and there
Ride on the pants triumphing!

                                        4.8.13–16

I come, my queen.

                                        4.14.51

          Shall I abide
In this dull world, which in thy absence is
No better than a sty?

                                        4.15.62–64

My master and my lord!

                                        5.2.189

As You Like It

Can I not say, 'I thank you'? My better parts
Are all thrown down, and that which here stands up
Is but a quintain, a mere lifeless block.

                                        1.2.239–41

What passion hangs these weights upon my tongue?

                                        1.2.247

I remember the kissing of [your] batler, and the cow's
    dugs that [your] pretty chopt hands had milked; and
    I remember the wooing of a peascod instead of [you],
    from whom I took two cods, and giving [you] them
    again, said with weeping tears, 'Wear these for my
    sake'.

2.4.45-51

What'er you are . . .
If ever from your eyelids wip'd a tear,
And know what 'tis to pity and be pitied,
Let gentleness my strong enforcement be;
In the which hope, I blush, and hide my sword.

2.7.109-19

[I play] the lover,
Sighing like a furnace, with a woeful ballad
Made to his mistress' eyebrow.

2.7.147-48

Hang there my verse, in witness of my love.

3.2.1

O [my beloved], these trees shall be my books,
And in their barks my thoughts I'll character,
That every eye which in this forest looks,
Shall see thy virtue witness'd everywhere.

3.2.5-8

Run, run . . . carve on every tree
The fair, the chaste, and unexpressive she.

3.2.9-10

Fair youth, I would I could make thee believe I love.

3.2.375-76

I am that he, that unfortunate he [that hangs verses on
   the trees].
                                        3.2.382–85

Neither rhyme nor reason can express how much [I am
   in love].
                                        3.2.387

You have heard [me] swear downright [I am in love].
                                        3.4.26

Do not scorn me. . . .
Say that you love me not, but say not so
In bitterness.
                                        3.5.1–3

If ever, as that ever may be near,
You meet in some fresh cheek the power of fancy,
Then shall you know the wounds invisible
That love's keen arrows make.
                                        3.5.28–31

[I've] fallen in love with your foulness.
                                        3.5.66

[I'll] fall in love with [your] anger.
                                        3.5.67

If you do sorrow at my grief in love,
By giving love, your sorrow and my grief
Were both extermined.
                                        3.5.87–89

      Loose now and then
A scatter'd smile, and that I'll live upon.
                                        3.5.103–4

I take some joy to say you are, [the one I love].
4.1.85

I protest [your] frown might kill me.
4.1.105

With pure love and troubled brain, [have I] . . . gone
    forth to sleep.
4.3.3–5

[You] say I am not fair, that I lack manners.
[You] call me proud, and that [you] could not love me,
Were man as rare as phoenix.
4.3.15–17

If the scorn of your bright eyne
Have power to raise such love in mine,
Alack, in me, what strange effect
Would they work in mild aspect?
4.3.50–53

Faithful offer take
Of me and all that I can make,
Or else . . . my love deny,
And then I'll study how to die.
4.3.60–65

O, how bitter a thing it is to look into happiness through
    another man's eyes!
5.2.42–44

I shall tomorrow be at the height of heart-heaviness, by
    how much I shall think [another] happy in having
    what he wishes for.
5.2.44–47

[To love] is to be all made of sighs and tears,
And so am I for [you].

5.2.83–84

[To love] is to be all made of faith and service,
And so am I for [you].

5.2.88–89

[To love] is to be all made of fantasy,
All made of passion and all made of wishes,
All adoration, duty and observance,
All humbleness, all patience and impatience,
All purity, all trial, all observance;
And so am I for [you].

5.2.93–98

Why blame you me to love you?

5.2.101–2

A poor virgin sir,
[I am] an ill-favoured thing sir, but [I am thine] own.

5.4.58

CYMBELINE

I profess myself [your] adorer, not [your] friend.

1.5.65–66

Most miserable
Is the desire that's glorious.

1.6.6–7

Even the very middle of my heart
Is warm'd by [you].

1.7.27–28

O dearest soul: your cause doth strike my heart
With pity that doth make me sick!

                    1.7.118–19

I have assail'd [you] with musics, but [you] vouchsafe
    no notice.

                    2.3.38–39

Still I swear I love you.

                    2.3.89

        What is it to be false?
To lie in watch there [in bed] and to think on [you]?
To weep 'twixt clock and clock?

                    3.4.41–43

        What is it to be false?
        . . . If sleep charge Nature,
To break it with a fearful dream of [you],
And [I] cry myself awake?

                    3.4.41–45

    Look,
I draw the sword myself, take it, and hit
The innocent mansion of my love, my heart:
Fear not, 'tis empty of all things, but grief:
[Thou art] not there, who was indeed
The riches of it.

                    3.4.67–73

        Now I think on thee,
My hunger's gone; but even before, I was
At point to sink, for food.

                    3.6.15–17

I am sick still, heart-sick.

4.2.37

Well, or ill, I am bound to you.

4.2.45–46

    Mine eyes
Were not in fault, for [you were] beautiful:
Mine ears that heard [your] flattery, nor my heart
That thought [you] like [you] seeming.

5.5.62–65

    The boy disdains me,
He leaves me, scorns me: briefly die their joys
That place them on the truth of girls and boys.

5.5.105–7

HAMLET

Perhaps [you] love [me] now,
And now no soil nor cautel doth besmirch
The virtue of [your] will; but [I] must fear.

1.3.14–16

I have not art to reckon my groans.

2.2.119–20

[I bear] the pangs of dispriz'd love.

3.1.72

The origin and commencement of [my] grief
Sprung from neglected love.

3.1.179–80

Now what my love is, proof hath made you know.

3.2.164

As my love is siz'd, my fear is so.

3.2.165

My lord, you once did love me.

3.2.326

Save me and hover o'er me with your wings.

3.4.104

Thou hast cleft my heart in twain.

3.4.158

[You] beat [my] heart.

4.5.5

What is the reason you use me thus?
I lov'd you ever.

5.1.284–85

Thou would'st not think how ill all's here about my
heart; but it is no matter.

5.2.208–9

If your mind dislike anything, obey it. I will forestall.

5.2.213

Let my disclaiming from a purpos'd evil
Free me so far in your most generous thoughts.

5.2.237–38

If thou didst ever hold me in thy heart,
Absent thee from felicity for awhile,
And in this harsh world draw thy breath in pain
To tell my story.

5.2.351–54

LOVE'S LABOUR'S LOST

Expecting thy reply, I profane my lips on thy foot, my
    eyes on thy picture, and my heart on thy every part.
                        4.1.84–86

Rebuke me not for that which you provoke.
                              5.2.347

O! I am yours, and all that I possess.
                              5.2.383

Here stand I, lady; dart thy skill at me;
Bruise me with scorn, confound me with a flout;
Thrust thy sharp wit quite through thy ignorance;
Cut me to pieces with thy keen conceit.
                         5.2.396–99

    Soft! let us see:
Write 'Lord have mercy on us' on those three;
They are infected, in their hearts it lies;
They have the plague, and caught it of your eyes.
                        5.2.418–21

I do adore thy sweet grace's slipper.
                             5.2.659

And what to me, my love? and what to me?
                             5.2.809

MEASURE FOR MEASURE

You do blaspheme the good, in mocking me.
                             1.4.38

I am a woeful suitor to your honour;
Please but your honour hear me.

                                    2.2.27–28

          O, think on that,
And mercy then will breathe within your lips,
Like man new made.

                                    2.2.77–79

At what hour tomorrow shall I attend your lordship?
                              2.2.160–61

When I think of [you] my gravity,
Wherein—let no man hear me—I take pride,
Could I with boot change for an idle plume
Which the air beats for vain.

                                    2.4.9–12

          O heavens,
Why does my blood thus muster to my heart,
Making both it unable for itself
And dispossessing all my other parts
Of necessary fitness?

                                    2.4.19–23

[I] crowd to [your] presence, where [my] untaught love
Must needs appear offence.

                                    2.4.28–29

O pardon me my lord; it oft falls out
To have what we would have, we speak not what we
     mean.

                                    2.4.117–18

I something do excuse the thing I hate
For his advantage that I dearly love.

                                    2.4.119–20

[You] cleave a heart in twain.

3.1.62

Why give you me this shame?

3.1.80

Marble to [my] tears, [you're] washed with them, but
relent not.

3.1.229–30

[I have] yet in [me] the continuance of [my] first
affection.

3.1.239–40

[Your] unjust unkindness, that in all reason should have
quenched [my] love, hath, like an impediment in the
current, made it more violent and unruly.

3.1.240–43

I have laboured for [you] to the extremest shore of my
modesty.

3.2.244–46

Shame to him whose cruel striking
Kills for faults of his own liking!

3.2.260–61

Take, o take those lips away
  that so sweetly were forsworn,
And those eyes, the break of day
  lights that do mislead the morn:
But my kisses bring again,
  bring again;
Seals of love, but seal'd in vain,
  seal'd in vain.

4.1.1–6

I am always bound to you.

4.1.25

But that [your] tender shame
Will not proclaim against [your] maiden loss,
How might [you] tongue me!

4.4.21–23

Hear me! O hear me, hear!

5.1.34

This is that face . . .
Which once thou swor'st was worth the looking on:
This is the hand which, with a vow'd contract,
Was fast belock'd in thine: this is the body
That . . . did supply thee at thy garden-house.

5.1.206–12

I am sorry one so learned and so wise
As you . . . have [always] appear'd,
Should slip so grossly, both in the heart of blood
And lack of temper'd judgment afterward.

5.1.468–71

THE MERRY WIVES OF WINDSOR

I shall never laugh but in [this] maid's company!

1.4.146

I will not say pity me—'tis not a soldier-like phrase—
   but I say, love me.

2.1.11–13

I have long loved [you] and . . . followed [you] with a
   doting observance; engrossed opportunities to meet

[you]; fee'd every slight occasion that could but
niggardly give me sight of [you].

2.2.188–92

[My love is] like a fair house built on another man's
ground, so that I have lost my edifice by mistaking
the place where I erected it.

2.2.209–11

Now shall I sin in my wish: I would thy husband were
dead; I'll speak it before the best lord: I would make
thee my lady.

3.3.43–45

I pray you pardon me; pray heartily pardon me.

3.3.210–11

[I'll] make you amends, I warrant you.

3.5.43

A MIDSUMMER NIGHT'S DREAM

[You] linger my desires,
Like to a step-dame or a dowager
Long withering out a young man's revenue.

1.1.4–6

[I am] a lover, that kills himself most gallant for love.

1.2.20

You draw me, you hard-hearted adamant—
But yet you draw not iron, for my heart
Is true as steel. Leave you your power to draw,
And I shall have no power to follow you.

2.1.195–98

I am your spaniel; . . .
The more you beat me, I will fawn on you.
Use me but as your spaniel, spurn me, strike me,
Neglect me, lose me; only give me leave,
Unworthy as I am, to follow you.

2.1.203–7

What worser place can I beg in your love—
And yet a place of high respect with me—
Than to be used as you use your dog?

2.1.208–10

Wherefore was I to this keen mockery born?
When at your hands did I deserve this scorn?

2.2.122–23

Good troth, you do me wrong, good sooth, you do,
In such disdainful manner me to woo.

2.2.128–29

What, out of hearing? Gone? No sound, no word?
Alack, where are you? Speak, and if you hear;
Speak, of all loves! I swoon almost with fear.

2.2.151–53

O why rebuke you him that loves you so?
Lay breath so bitter on your bitter foe.

3.2.43–44

So should the murder'd look, and so should I,
Pierc'd through the heart with your stern cruelty;
Yet you, the murderer, look as bright, as clear,
As yonder Venus in her glimmering sphere.

3.2.58–61

All fancy-sick [I am], and pale of cheer
With sighs of love, that costs the fresh blood dear.
3.2.96–97

Why are you grown so rude? What change is this,
Sweet love?
3.2.262–63

I am as fair now as I was erewhile.
Since night you lov'd me; yet since night you left me.
3.2.274–75

What, wilt thou hear some music, my sweet love?
4.1.27

Say, sweet love, what thou desir'st to eat?
4.1.30

O how I love thee! How I dote on thee!
4.1.44

MUCH ADO ABOUT NOTHING

I do love nothing in the world so well as you—is not
    that strange?
4.1.266–67

By my sword . . . thou lovest me . . . I will swear by it
    that you love me, and I will make him eat it that says
    I love not you.
4.1.273, 275–76

I love you with so much of my heart that none is left to
    protest.
4.1.285–86

'Suffer love'—a good epithet! I do suffer love indeed, for I
  love thee against my will.
                                        5.2.62–63

I will live in thy heart, die in thy lap, and be buried in thy
  eyes; and moreover, I will go with thee to thy uncle's.
                                        5.2.94–96

OTHELLO

I will wear my heart upon my sleeve.
                                        1.1.63

[I am] in chains of magic . . . bound.
                                        1.2.65

Thou hast practised on [me] with foul charms,
Abused [my] delicate youth with drugs or minerals
That weakens motion.
                                        1.2.73–75

        My heart's subdued
Even to the very quality of [you].
                                        1.3.251–52

It is a silliness to live when to live is torment;
        and then have we a prescription to die, when death is
        our physician.
                                        1.3.309–11

        O my sweet,
I prattle out of fashion, and I dote
In mine own comforts [from seeing you].
                                        2.1.204–6

Love hath turned [me] almost the wrong side out.

2.3.49

[My] soul is so enfettered to [your] love
That [you] may make, unmake, do what [you] list,
Even as [your] appetite shall play the god
With [me].

2.3.340–43

     Perdition catch my soul
But I do love thee! and when I love thee not
Chaos is come again.

3.3.90–92

I humbly do beseech you of your pardon
For too much loving you.

3.3.215–16

     I do beseech you
That by your virtuous means I may again
Exist, and be a member of [your] love
Whom I, with all the office of my heart
Entirely honour.

3.4.111–15

[I am] a creature that dotes on [you].

4.1.96–97

I never knew a woman love man so.

4.1.111

[You] haunt me in every place.

4.1.132–33

     I would do much
T'atone [us], for the love I bear [you].

4.1.231–32

I will not stay to offend you.

4.1.246

[In you] I have garnered up my heart.

4.2.58

Either I must live [in you] or bear no life.

4.2.59

[You are] the fountain from the which my current runs
Or else dries up.

4.2.60–61

Alas, what ignorant sin have I committed?

4.2.71

If e'er my will did trespass 'gainst [your] love
Either in discourse of thought or actual deed,
Or that mine eyes, mine ears or any sense
Delighted them in any other form,
Or that I do not yet, and ever did,
And ever will—though [you] do shake me off
To beggarly divorcement—love [you] dearly,
Comfort forswear me!

4.2.154–61

>   Unkindness may do much,
> And [your] unkindness may defeat my life
> But never taint my love.

4.2.161–63

>   My love doth so approve [you]
> That even [your] stubbornness, [your] cheeks, [your]
>   frowns
> . . . have grace and favour.

4.3.17–19

PERICLES

You gods, that made me man, and sway in love,
That have inflam'd desire in my breast
To taste the fruit of yon celestial tree
Or die in the adventure, be my helps,
As I am son and servant to your will,
To compass such a boundless happiness!

I.I.20–25

[I am a] martyr slain in Cupid's wars.

I.I.39

[I bequeath] my unspotted fire of love to you.

I.I.54

My heart can lend no succour to my head.

I.Ib.171

[You] make . . . my body pine and soul to languish.

I.2.33

Pardon me, or strike me, if you please;
I cannot be much lower than my knees.

I.2.47–48

I never did [you] hurt in all my life.
I never spake bad word, nor did ill turn
To any living creature; believe me la,
I never kill'd a mouse, nor hurt a fly.

4.1.74–77

I have cried [you] almost to the number of [your] hairs;
I have drawn [your] picture with my voice.

4.2.91–92

[I] speak,
. . . [as one] that, may be, hath endur'd a grief
Might equal yours, if both were justly weigh'd.
5.1.86–88

ROMEO AND JULIET

Many a morning [have I] there been seen,
With tears augmenting the fresh morning's dew,
Adding to clouds more clouds with [my] deep sighs.
1.1.129–31

Not having that which, having, makes [hours] short
[Is being] out of [your] favour where I am in love.
1.1.162–65

Alas that love so gentle in his view
Should be so tyrannous and rough in proof.
1.1.166–67

[I weep] at thy good heart's oppression.
1.1.182

Soft, I will go along;
And if you leave me so, you do me wrong.
1.1.193–94

[You are] too fair, too wise, wisely too fair,
To merit bliss by making me despair.
1.1.219–20

[You have] forsworn to love, and in that vow
Do I live dead, that live to tell it now.
1.1.221–22

I am too sore enpierced with [Cupid's] shaft
To soar with his light feathers.

1.4.19–20

[I am] so bound
I cannot bound a pitch above dull woe.
Under love's heavy burden do I sink.

1.4.20–22

The game was ne'er so fair and I am done.

1.4.39

Romeo! Humours! Madman! Passion! Lover!
Appear thou in the likeness of a sigh,
Speak but one rhyme and I am satisfied.

2.1.7–9

Call me but love, and I'll be new baptis'd.

2.2.50

If thou dost love, pronounce it faithfully.
Or, if thou think'st I am too quickly won,
I'll frown and be perverse and say thee nay,
So thou wilt woo; but else, not for the world.

2.2.94–97

In truth . . . I am too fond,
And therefore thou mayst think my haviour light,
But trust me gentleman, I'll prove more true
Than those that have more cunning to be strange.

2.2.98–101

I should have been more strange, I must confess,
But that thou overheard'st, ere I was ware,
My true-love passion.

2.2.102–4

Whining and Wheedling | 257

Swear by thy gracious self,
Which is the god of my idolatry,
And I'll believe thee.

2.2.113–15

[Grant] th'exchange of thy love's faithful vow for mine.

2.2.127

I gave thee [my love's faithful vow] before thou did'st
    request it,
And yet I would it were to give again . . .
But to be frank and give it thee again.

2.2.128–31

I wish but for the thing I have.

2.2.132

If that thy bent of love be honourable,
Thy purpose marriage, send me word tomorrow . . .
Where and what time thou wilt perform the rite.

2.2.143–46

        If thou meanest not well
I do beseech thee . . .
To cease thy strife and leave me to my grief.

2.2.150–52

I would I were thy bird.

2.2.182

Plainly know my heart's dear love is set
On [you].

2.3.53–54

Thou chid'st me oft . . .
For doting, not for loving.

2.3.77–78

[You] pale, hard-hearted wench that . . . torments [me]
so that [I] will sure run mad.

2.4.4–5

[I am] already dead, stabbed with a white wench's black
eye, run through the ear with a love song, the very
pin of [my] heart cleft with the blind bow-boy's butt-
shaft.

2.4.13–16

My wit faints.

2.4.69

Afore God I am so vexed that every part about me
quivers.

2.4.158–59

Let me tell ye, if ye should lead [me] in a fool's
paradise . . . it were a very gross kind of behaviour.

2.4.162–64

[I am] young, and therefore, if you should deal double
with [me], truly it were an ill thing . . . and very weak
dealing.

2.4.165–67

[I] love thee better than thou canst devise
Till thou shalt know the reason of my love.

3.1.68–69

O, what a beast was I to chide at [you].

3.2.95

Ah, poor my lord, what tongue shall smooth thy name
When I thy three-hours wife have mangled it?

3.2.98–99

Thou cut'st my head off with a golden axe
And smilest upon the stroke that murders me.

                    3.3.22–23

Art thou gone so? Love, lord, ay husband, friend,
I must hear from thee every day in the hour,
For in a minute there are many days.
O, by this count I shall be much in years
Ere I again behold [you].

                    3.5.43–47

Farewell.
I will omit no opportunity
That may convey my greetings, love, to thee.

                    3.5.48–50

Alack, alack, that heaven should practise stratagems
Upon so soft a subject as myself.

                    3.5.209–10

If I [confess I love you] it will be of more price
Being spoke behind your back than to your face.

                    4.1.27–28

Love give me strength.

                    4.1.125

By heaven I love thee better than myself.

                    5.3.64

The Taming of the Shrew

I burn, I pine, I perish,
If I achieve not this young modest girl.
                              1.1.155–56

Let me be a slave, t'achieve that maid
Whose sudden sight hath thrall'd my wounded eye.
                              1.1.219–20

O, put me in thy books.

                              2.1.222

I am one that loves [you] more
Than words can witness or your thoughts can guess.
                              2.1.328–29

Show pity or I die.

                              3.1.76

The Tempest

I have done nothing but in care of thee,
Of thee, my dear one.
                              1.2.16–17

I prithee,
Remember I have done thee worthy service;
Told thee no lies, made no mistakings, serv'd
Without grudge or grumblings.
                              1.2.246–49

My affections
Are then most humble; I have no ambition
To see a goodlier man.
                              1.2.484–86

Might I but through my prison once a day
Behold [you]: all corners else o' th' earth
Let liberty make use of; space enough
Have I in such a prison.

1.2.493–96

I will kiss thy foot: I prithee, be my god.

2.2.149

Hear my soul speak:
The very instant that I saw you, did
My heart fly to your service; there resides,
To make me slave to it.

3.1.63–66

Do you love me?

3.1.67

I am a fool to weep at what I am glad of.

3.1.73–74

[I weep] at mine unworthiness.

3.1.79

  Hence, bashful cunning!
And prompt me plain and holy innocence!
I am your wife if you will marry me;
If not, I'll die your maid: to be your fellow
You may deny me; but I'll be your servant,
Whether you will or no.

3.1.81–86

[Be] my mistress, dearest;
And I thus humble ever.

3.1.86–87

[I'll be thy husband] with a heart as willing
As bondage e'er of freeedom: here's my hand.

3.1.88–89

[Here's my hand], with my heart in 't.

3.1.90

If you now beheld [me], your affections
Would become tender.

5.1.18–19

Now my charms are all o'er thrown,
And what strength I have's mine own,
Which is most faint.

Epilogue.1–3

TROILUS AND CRESSIDA

I am weaker than a woman's tear,
Tamer than sleep, fonder than ignorance,
Less valiant than the virgin in the night,
And skilless as unpractis'd infancy.

1.1.9–12

      My heart,
As wedged with a sigh, would rive in twain.

1.1.34–35

Lest [any other people] should perceive me,
I have, as when the sun doth light a storm,
Buried this sigh in wrinkle of a smile;
But sorrow that is couch'd in seeming gladness
Is like that mirth fate turns to sudden sadness.

1.1.36–40

When I do tell thee there my hopes lie drown'd,
Reply not in how many fathoms deep
They lie indrench'd.

1.1.49–51

I tell thee I am mad
In [your] love: thou answer'st, '[I] am fair';
Pour'st in the open ulcer of my heart
[Your] eyes, [your] hair, [your] cheek, [your] gait,
     [your] voice.

1.1.51–54

But saying thus, instead of oil and balm,
Thou lay'st in every gash that love hath given me
The knife that made it.

1.1.61–63

There is no lady of more softer bowels,
More spongy to suck in the sense of fear,
More ready to cry out 'Who knows what follows?'

2.2.11–13

I stalk about [your] door
Like a strange soul upon the Stygian banks
Staying for waftage.

3.2.7–9

Boldness comes to me now, and brings me heart:
     . . . I have lov'd you night and day
For many weary months.

3.2.112–14

Hard to seem won; but I was won, my lord,
With the first glance that ever—Pardon me:
If I confess much you will play the tyrant.
I love you now, but till now not so much
But I might master it. In faith I lie—

My thoughts were like unbridled children, grown
Too headstrong for their mother.

3.2.116–22

Though I lov'd you well, I woo'd you not.

3.2.125

Sweet, bid me hold my tongue,
For in this rapture I shall surely speak
The thing I shall repent.

3.2.128–30

Your silence,
Cunning in dumbness, from my weakness draws
My very soul of counsel. Stop my mouth.

3.2.130–32

Never did young man fancy
With so eternal and so fix'd a soul.

5.2.164–65

TWELFTH NIGHT

[I will]
Make me a willow cabin at your gate,
And call upon my soul within the house;
Write loyal cantons of contemned love,
And sing them loud even in the dead of night;
Halloo your name to the reverberate hills,
And make the babbling gossip of the air
Cry out [your name]. O, you should not rest
Between the elements of air and earth,
But you should pity me.

1.5.272–79

If you will not murder me for my love, let me be your
    servant.

                    2.1.34–35

Jove I thank thee, I will smile, I will do every thing that
    you thou wilt have me.

                    2.5.178–79

Shall I play my freedom at try-trip, and become thy
    bond-slave?

                    2.5.190–91

My duty, madam, and most humble service.

                    3.1.97

        'Twas never merry world
Since lowly feigning was call'd compliment.

                    3.1.100–101

Your servant's servant is your servant, madam.

                    3.1.104

Give me leave, beseech you.

                    3.1.113

        I did send,
After the last enchantment you did here,
A ring in chase of you. So did I abuse
Myself, my servant, and, I fear me, you.

                    3.1.113–16

Under your hard construction must I sit.

                    3.1.117

What might you think?
Have you not set mine honour at the stake,
And baited it with all th' unmuzzled thoughts
That tyrannous heart can think?

3.1.119–22

To one of your receiving
Enough is shown; a cypress, not a bosom,
Hides my heart: so, let me hear you speak.

3.1.122–24

[Your] commands shall be executed.

3.4.27

Plight me the full assurance of your faith,
That my most jealous and too doubtful soul
May live at peace.

4.3.26–28

You uncivil lady,
To whose ingrate and unauspicious altars
My soul the faithfull'st off'rings hath breath'd out
That e'er devotion tender'd—What shall I do?

5.1.110–13

THE TWO GENTLEMEN OF VERONA

On a love-book pray for my success.

1.1.19

[I am] over boots in love.

1.1.25

I leave myself, my friends, and all, for love.

1.1.65

Thou hast metamorphos'd me;
Made me neglect my studies, lose my time,
War with good counsel, set the world at nought;
Made wit with musing weak, heart sick with thought.
                          1.1.66–69

O hateful hands, to tear such loving words;
Injurious wasps, to feed on such sweet honey,
And kill the bees that yield it, with your stings!
                          1.2.106–8

When that hour o'erslips me in the day
Wherein I sigh not . . . for thy sake,
The next ensuing hour some foul mischance
Torment me for my love's forgetfulness.
                          2.2.9–12

I have done penance for contemning Love,
Whose high imperious thoughts have punish'd me
With bitter fasts, with penitential groans,
With nightly tears, and daily heart-sore sighs.
                          2.4.124–27

For in revenge of my contempt of Love,
Love hath chas'd sleep from my enthralled eyes,
And made them watchers of mine own heart's sorrow.
                          2.4.128–30

Love's a mighty lord,
And hath so humbled me, as I confess
There is no woe to his correction,
Nor to his service, no such joy on earth.
                          2.4.131–34

[I am] dignified with this high honour,
To bear my lady's train, lest the base earth
Should from her vesture chance to steal a kiss,
And of so great a favour growing proud,
Disdain to root the summer-swelling flower,
And make rough winter everlastingly.

                                        2.4.153–58

I love this lady too-too much.

                                        2.4.201

How shall I dote on [you] with more advice,
That thus without advice begin to love [you]?

                                        2.4.202–4

Love bade me swear, and Love bids me forswear.

                                        2.6.6

A true-devoted pilgrim is not weary
To measure kingdoms with his feeble steps,
Much less shall she that hath Love's wings to fly,
And when the flight is made to one so dear,
Of such divine perfection as [you].

                                        2.7.9–13

O, know'st thou not [your] looks are my soul's food?
Pity the dearth that I have pined in,
By longing for that food so long a time.

                                        2.7.15–17

(For long agone I have forgot to court,
Besides the fashion of the time is chang'd)
How and which way may I bestow myself
To be regarded in [your] sun-bright eye?

                                        3.1.87–88

Notwithstanding all [your] sudden quips,
The least whereof would quell a lover's hope,
Yes, spaniel-like, the more [you] spurn my love,
The more it grows, and fawneth on [you] still.

4.2.12–15

[I] loved [you] out of all nick.

4.2.72–73

[I] dream on [you] that has forgot [my] love.

4.4.81

Alas, how love can trifle with itself!

4.4.181

O thou that dost inhabit my breast,
Leave not the mansion so long tenantless,
Lest growing ruinous, the building fall,
And leave no memory of what it was.
Repair me, with thy presence: . . .
Thou gentle nymph, cherish thy forlorn swain.

5.4.7–11

O 'tis the curse in love, and still approv'd,
When women cannot love where they're belov'd.

5.4.43–44

THE WINTER'S TALE

There is no tongue that moves, none, none i' th' world,
So soon as yours, could win me.

1.2.20–21

I am yours forever.

1.2.105

I cannot be
Mine own, nor anything to any, if
I be not thine.

4.4.43−45

Heart-throbbing

FLORID LOVE POETRY is the pure stuff of popular Shakespeare. People can't help falling for it and can't get enough. His love poems simply work. Even on you.

Take advantage of the truth that everyone is basically tuned in to rhythm and rhyme. It's embedded in the brain from the heartbeat and breathing. Poetry is the official language of the human body. People perk up when what sounds like poetry pops up in ordinary conversation.

Shakespeare makes his poetry fit the moment. Kings get lots of noble poetry—to keep their subjects in thrall to divine pleasure. Peasants get prose. Bad poetry mocks the pretentious, like the young King of Navarre reeling off pompous drivel. And Romeo! How can you tell he's got the wrong girl at the beginning of the play? Terrible poetry, which suddenly changes when he runs into Juliet. Not to mention Orlando abusing the trees with greeting-card verses to Ros. Still, it's poetry. And for better or worse, Orlando and Rosalind end up married.

Poetry takes the long way around to get someplace very near—just like seduction. Indeed, the two are nearly the same thing. Poetry makes you notice things. It can make somebody notice you. Get ready.

This chapter gives you the ultimate heart-blinding lines. Here's persuasion-by-the-page. Allure-between-covers. Golden-tonguing and sweet-talking. Some of it's as fine as anything ever spoken. Some is a joke. But all of it has seduction written all over it.

All's Well That Ends Well

What power is it which mounts my love so high,
That makes me see, and cannot feed mine eye?
                                        1.1.216–17

I grow to you, and our parting is a tortur'd body.
                                        2.1.36

A heaven on earth I have won by wooing thee.
                                        4.2.66

Antony and Cleopatra

Eternity was in our lips and eyes,
Bliss in our brows' bent; none our parts so poor
But was a race of heaven. They are so still.
                                        1.3.36–38

I here importune death awhile until
Of many thousand kisses the poor last
I lay upon thy lips.
                                        4.15.20–22

As You Like It

The truth of thy love to me [is] so righteously tempered
    as mine is to thee.
                                        1.2.12–13

Let your fair eyes and gentle wishes go with me.
                                        1.2.174–75

    We still [will sleep] together,
Rise at an instant, learn, play, eat together,

And whereso'er we go, like Juno's swans,
Still we go coupled and inseparable.

1.3.69–73

From the east to western Inde,
No jewel is like Rosalind.

3.2.86–87

Her worth being mounted on the wind,
Through all the world bears Rosalind.

3.2.88–89

All the pictures fairest lin'd
Are but black to Rosalind.

3.2.90–91

Let no face be kept in mind
But the fair of Rosalind.

3.2.92–93

If hart do lack a hind,
Let him seek out Rosalind.

3.2.99–100

If the cat will after kind,
So be sure will Rosalind.

3.2.101–2

Winter'd garments must be lin'd,
So must slender Rosalind.

3.2.103–4

They that reap must sheaf and bind,
Then to cart with Rosalind.

3.2.105–6

Sweetest nut hath sourest rind,
Such a nut is Rosalind.

3.2.107–8

He that sweetest rose will find
Must find love's prick, and Rosalind.

3.2.109–110

Nature presently distill'd
Helen's cheek, but not her heart,
Cleopatra's majesty,
Atalanta's better part,
Sad Lucretia's modesty.
Thus Rosalind of many parts
By heavenly synod was devis'd,
Of many faces, eyes, and hearts,
To have the touches dearest priz'd.
Heaven would that she these gifts should have,
And I to live and die her slave.

3.2.141–51

So holy and so perfect is my love,
And I in such a poverty of grace,
That I shall think it a most plenteous crop
To glean the broken ears after the man
That the main harvest reaps.

3.5.99–103

[We] are in the very wrath of love, and [we] will
together. Clubs cannot part [us].

5.2.39–40

It was a lover and his lass,
With a hey and a ho and a hey nonino,
That o'er the green corn-field did pass,
In spring-time the only pretty ring-time,

When birds do sing, hey ding a ding, ding,
Sweet lovers love the spring.

Between the acres of the rye,
    With a hey and a ho and a hey nonino,
These pretty country-folks would lie,
    In spring-time, the only pretty ring-time,
When birds do sing, hey ding a ding, ding,
Sweet lovers love the spring.

This carol they began that hour,
    With a hey and a ho and a hey nonino,
How that a life was but a flower,
    In spring-time, the only pretty ring-time,
When birds do sing, hey ding a ding, ding,
Sweet lovers love the spring.

And therefore take the present time,
    With a hey and a ho and a hey nonino,
For love is crowned with the prime,
    In spring-time, the only pretty ring-time,
When birds do sing, hey ding a ding, ding,
Sweet lovers love the spring.

5.3.13–37

[I would have you,] were I of all kingdoms king.
5.4.10

[I would have you,] though to have [you] and death
    were both one thing.
5.4.17

You and [I] no cross shall part.
5.4.130

You and {I} are heart in heart.

5.4.131

Wedding is great Juno's crown,
O blessed bond of board of bed.
'Tis Hymen peoples every town;
High wedlock then be honoured.

5.4.140–43

CYMBELINE

I shall here abide . . . comforted . . . that there is this
 jewel in the world that I may see again.

1.2.20–23

  Write my queen,
And with mine eyes I'll drink the words you send,
Though ink be made of gall.

1.2.30–32

  The flame o' th' taper
Bows toward {you}, and would under-peep {your} lids,
To see th' enclosed lights, now canopied
Under these windows, white and azure lac'd
With blue of heaven's own tinct.

2.2.19–23

  On {your} left breast
A mole cinque-spotted: like the crimson drops
I' th' bottom of a cowslip.

2.2.37–39

O, learn'd indeed were that astronomer
That knew the stars as I {your} characters;
He'd lay the future open.

3.2.27–29

Let what is here contain'd relish of love.

3.2.30

Wing'd with fervour of [my] love, [I've] flown
To [you].

3.5.62–63

Flow, flow,
You heavenly blessings, on [my love]!

3.5.161–62

I love thee: I have spoke it.

4.2.16

Nobly [I] yoke
A smiling with a sigh; as if the sigh
Was that it was, for not being such a smile.

4.2.51–53

O sweetest, fairest lily.

4.2.201

HAMLET

The head is not more native to the heart,
The hand more instrumental to the mouth,
Than [I shall be to you].

1.2.47–49

[Your] gentle and unforc'd accord . . .
Sits smiling to my heart.

1.2.123–24

[You are] as watchman to my heart.

1.3.46

This is the very ecstasy of love,
Whose violent property fordoes itself
And leads the will to desperate undertakings
As oft as any passion under heaven
That does afflict our natures.

2.1.102–6

Doubt thou the stars are fire,
Doubt that the sun doth move,
Doubt truth to be a liar,
But never doubt I love.

2.2.115–18

I love thee best, O most best, believe it.

2.2.120–21

[I cannot] give my heart a winking mute and dumb,
Or look upon this love with idle sight.

2.2.137–38

Your good beauties [are] the happy cause
Of [my] wildness.

3.1.39–40

[You gave me gifts] and with them words of so sweet
   breath compos'd
As made the things more rich.

3.1.98–99

Since my dear soul was mistress of her choice,
And could of men distinguish her election,
Sh'ath seal'd thee for herself.

3.2.63–65

Many journeys may the sun and moon
Make us again count o'er ere love be done.

3.2.156–57

Where love is great, the littlest doubts are fear;
Where little fears grow great, great love grows there.

                                        3.2.166–67

Never come mischance between us twain.

                                        3.2.223

Tomorrow is Saint Valentine's day,
    All in the morning betime,
And I a maid at your window,
    To be your Valentine.

                                        4.5.48–51

Nature is fine in love.

                                        4.5.161

[You are] so conjunctive to my life and soul
That, as the star moves not but in his sphere,
I could not but by [you].

                                        4.7.14–16

I do receive your offer'd love like love
And will not wrong it.

                                        5.2.247–48

          Good night, sweet prince,
And flights of angels sing thee to thy rest.

                                        5.2.364–65

LOVE'S LABOUR'S LOST

I love thee.

                                        1.2.132

If love make me forsworn, how shall I swear to love?
Ah! never faith could hold, if not to beauty vow'd;

Though to myself forsworn, to thee I'll faithful prove:
Those thoughts to me were oaks, to thee like osiers bow'd.
Study his bias leaves and make his book thine eyes,
Where all those pleasures live that art would comprehend.
If knowledge be the mark, to know thee shall suffice;
Well learned is that tongue that well can thee commend;
All ignorant that soul that sees thee without wonder;
Which is to me some praise that I thy parts admire.
Thy eye Jove's lightning bears, thy voice his dreadful
       thunder,
Which, not to anger bent, is music and sweet fire.
Celestial as thou art, O! pardon love this wrong,
That sings heaven's praise with such an earthly tongue.

                                        4.2.101–14

So sweet a kiss the golden sun gives not
To those fresh morning drops upon the rose,
As thy eye-beams when their fresh rays have smote
The night of dew that on my cheeks down flows:
Nor shines the silver moon one half so bright
Through the transparent bosom of the deep,
As doth thy face through tears of mine give light
Thou shin'st in every tear that I do weep:
No drop but as a coach doth carry thee;
So ridest thou triumphing in my woe.
Do but behold the tears that swell in me,
And they thy glory through my grief will show:
But do not love thyself; then thou will keep
My tears for glasses, and still make me weep.
O queen of queens! how far dost thou excel,
No thought can think, nor tongue of mortal tell.

                                        4.3.24–39

Did not the heavenly rhetoric of thine eye,
'Gainst whom the world cannot hold argument,
Persuade my heart to this false perjury?

Vows for thee broke deserve not punishment.
A woman I forswore; but I will prove,
Thou being a goddess, I forswore not thee:
My vow was earthly, thou a heavenly love;
Thy grace being gain'd cures all disgrace in me.
Vows are but breath, and breath a vapour is:
Then thou, fair sun, which on my earth dost shine,
Exhal'st this vapour-vow; in thee it is:
If broken then, it is no fault of mine:
If by me broke, what fool is not so wise
To lose an oath to win a paradise?

4.3.57–70

On a day, alack the day!
Love, whose month is ever May,
Spied a blossom passing fair
Playing in the wanton air:
Through the velvet leaves the wind,
All unseen can passage find;
That the lover, sick to death,
Wish'd himself the heaven's breath.
Air, quoth he, thy cheeks may blow;
Air, would I might triumph so!
But alack! my hand is sworn
Ne'er to pluck thee from thy thorn:
Vow, alack! for youth unmeet,
Youth so apt to pluck a sweet.
Do not call it sin in me,
That I am forsworn for thee;
Thou for whom Jove would swear
Juno but an Ethiop were;
And deny himself for Jove,
Turning mortal for love.

4.3.98–117

Henceforth my wooing mind shall be express'd
In russet yeas and honest kersey noes:
And, to begin: Wench,—so God help me, law!—
My love to thee is sound, sans crack or flaw.

                              5.2.412–15

For your fair sake have [I] neglected time,
Play'd foul play with [my] oaths. Your beauty . . .
Hath much deform'd [me], fashioning [my] humours
Even to the opposed end of [my] intents.

                              5.2.747–50

Now, at the latest minute of the hour,
Grant [me] your love.

                              5.2.779–80

If this, or more than this, I would deny,
To flatter up these powers of mine with rest,
The sudden hand of death close up mine eye!

                              5.2.805–7

THE MERRY WIVES OF WINDSOR

Sir, the maid loves you, and all shall be well.

                              1.4.115

Let it suffice thee . . . —at the least, if the love of soldier
    can suffice—that I love thee.

                              2.1.9–11

Clap on more sails, pursue; up with [our] fights;
Give fire; [you] are my prize, or ocean whelm [us] all!

                              2.2.131–32

I have pursued [you] as love hath pursued me; which
  have been on the wing of all occasions.
                                        2.2.194–96

[You] dwell so securely on the excellency of [your]
  honour that the folly of my soul dares not present
  itself; too bright to be looked against.
                                        2.2.233–36

Come, I cannot cog and say thou art this and that, like a
  many of these lisping hawthorn-buds that come like
  women in men's apparel, and smell like Bucklersbury
  in simple time; I cannot; but I love thee, none but
  thee; and thou deserv'st it.
                                        3.3.63–68

          For that I love [you]
In such a righteous fashion as I do,
Perforce, against all checks, rebukes and manners,
I must advance the colours of my love,
And not retire. Let me have your good will.
                                        3.4.76–80

A MIDSUMMER NIGHT'S DREAM

I swear to thee by Cupid's strongest bow,
By his best arrow with the golden head,
By the simplicity of Venus' doves,
By that which knitteth souls and prospers loves,
And by that fire which burn'd the Carthage queen
When the false Trojan under sail was seen;
By all the vows that ever men have broke
(In number more than ever women spoke),

In that same place thou hast appointed me,
Tomorrow truly will I meet with thee.

1.1.169–78

Your virtue is my privilege: for that
It is not night when I do see your face,
Therefore I think I am not in the night;
Nor doth this wood lack worlds of company,
For you, in my respect, are all the world;
Then how can it be said I am alone,
When all the world is here to look on me?

2.1.220–26

I'll follow thee, and make a heaven of hell.

2.1.243

I mean that my heart unto yours is knit,
So that but one heart we can make of it.

2.2.46–47

Thy love ne'er alter till thy sweet life end!

2.2.60

Transparent [one]! Nature shows art,
That through thy bosom makes me see my heart.

2.2.103–4

Reason becomes the marshal to my will,
And leads me to your eyes, where I o'erlook
Love's stories, written in love's richest book.

2.2.119–21

When [my] love [I] doth espy,
Let her shine as gloriously
As the Venus of the sky.

3.2.105–7

O let me kiss
This princess of pure white, this seal of bliss!
                    3.2.143–44

I love thee, by my life I do;
I swear by that which I will lose for thee
To prove him false that says I love thee not.
                    3.2.251–53

Come sit thee down upon this flowery bed,
While I thy amiable cheeks do coy,
And stick musk-roses in thy sleep smooth head,
And kiss thy fair large ears, my gentle joy.
                    4.1.1–4

Like a sickness did I loathe this food:
But as in health, come to my natural taste,
Now I do wish it, love it, long for it,
And will for evermore be true to it.
                    4.1.172–75

I have found [you] like a jewel,
Mine own, and not mine own.
                    4.1.190–91

It seems to me
That yet we sleep, we dream.
                    4.1.191–93

Love, therefore, and tongue-tied simplicity
In least speak most, to my capacity.
                    5.1.104–5

My love thou art, my love I think!
                    5.1.192

Think what thou wilt, I am thy lover's grace.

5.1.193

MEASURE FOR MEASURE

What do I love [you]
That I desire to hear [you] speak again?
And feast upon [your] eyes? What is't I dream on?

2.2.177–79

[You surpass] heaven in my mouth.

2.4.4

Plainly conceive, I love you.

2.4.140

I know [you] and I love [you].

3.2.145

As there comes light from heaven, and words from
   breath,
As there is sense in truth, and truth in virtue
I am affianc'd this man's wife, as strongly
As words could make up vows.

5.1.224–27

For your lovely sake
Give me your hand and say you will be mine.

5.1.489–90

MUCH ADO ABOUT NOTHING

That I love [you], I feel.
That [you] are worthy, I know.

1.1.211–12

OTHELLO

I, observing,
Took once a pliant hour and found good means
To draw from [you] a prayer of earnest heart.
1.3.151–53

I saw [your] visage in [your] mind,
And to [your] honours and [your] valiant parts
Did I my soul and fortunes consecrate.
1.3.253–55

If it were now to die
'Twere now to be most happy, for I fear
My soul hath her content so absolute
That not another comfort like [seeing you now]
Succeeds in unknown fate.
2.1.187–91

I cannot speak enough of this content,
It stops me here, it is too much of joy.
2.1.194–95

When [you] speak is it not an alarum to love?
2.3.24

This crack of [our] love shall grow stronger than it was
    before.
2.3.319–20

PERICLES

With a soul
Embolden'd with the glory of [your] praise,
[I] think death no hazard in this enterprise.
1.1.3–5

[Your] face, like heaven, enticeth [me] to view
[Your] countless glory.

1.1.31–32

[With you I] feed on sweetest flowers.

1.1.33–34

Hope, succeeding from so fair a tree
As you fair self, doth tune us.

1.1.115

The passions of the mind,
That have their first conception by mis-dread,
Have after-nourishment and life by care.

1.2.12–14

Joy and all comfort in your sacred breast!

1.2.35

Lux tua vita mihi. [Thy light is life to me.]

2.2.21

Behold, [your] eyelids, cases to those
Heavenly jewels . . .
Begin to part their fringes of bright gold.
The diamonds of a most praised water
Doth appear to make the world twice rich.

3.2.100–104

Strike me, . . .
Give me a gash, put me to present pain,
Lest this great sea of joys rushing upon me
O'er bear the shores of my mortality,
And drown me with their sweetness.

5.1.190–94

Romeo and Juliet

O brawling love, O loving hate,
O anything of nothing first create!
O heavy lightness, serious vanity,
Misshapen chaos of well-seeming forms!
Feather of lead, bright smoke, cold fire, sick health,
Still-waking sleep that is not what it is!
This love feel I, that feel no love in this.

1.1.174–80

Love is a smoke made with the fume of sighs;
Being purg'd, a fire sparkling in lovers' eyes;
Being vex'd, a sea nourish'd with lovers' tears;
What is it else? A madness most discreet,
A choking gall, and a preserving sweet.

1.1.188–92

[You] will not stay the siege of loving terms
Nor bide th'encounter of assailing eyes
Nor ope [your] lap to saint-seducing gold;
O [you are] rich in beauty, only poor
That when [you] die, with beauty dies [your] store.

1.1.210–14

[You] earth-treading star that make dark heaven light.

1.2.25

    'Tis much pride
For fair without the fair within to hide.
That book in many's eyes doth share the glory
That in gold clasps locks in the golden story.

1.3.89–92

You are a lover, borrow Cupid's wings
And soar with them above a common bound.

1.4.17–18

[You] gallop night by night
Through lovers' brains, and then they dream of love.
                    1.4.70–71

If I profane with my unworthiest hand
This holy shrine, the gentle sin is this:
My lips, two blushing pilgrims, ready stand
To smooth that rough touch with a tender kiss.
                    1.5.92–95

[You are] my only love sprung from my only hate.
                    1.5.137

Passion lends [us] power, time means, to meet,
Tempering extremities with extreme sweet.
                    2.Prologue.13–14

But soft, what light through yonder window breaks?
It is the east and Juliet is the sun!
                    2.2.2–3

Arise fair sun and kill the envious moon
Who is already sick and pale with grief
That thou her maid art far more fair than she.
                    2.2.4–6

'Tis not to me [you] speak,
Two of the fairest stars in all the heaven,
Having some business, do entreat [your] eyes
To twinkle in their spheres till they return.
                    2.2.14–17

What if [your] eyes were there, [those stars] in [your]
    head?
The brightness of [your] cheek would shame those stars
As daylight doth a lamp. [Your] eyes in heaven

Would through the airy region stream so bright
That birds would sing and think it were not night.
2.2.18–22

See how [you] lean [your] cheek upon [your] hand.
O that I were a glove upon that hand,
That I might touch that cheek.
2.2.23–26

For thou art
As glorious to this night, being o'er my head,
As is a winged messenger of heaven
Unto the white-upturned wondering eyes
Of mortals that fall back to gaze on him
When he bestrides the lazy-puffing clouds
And sails upon the bosom of the air.
2.2.26–32

O Romeo, Romeo, wherefore art thou Romeo?
2.2.33

Doff thy name,
And for thy name, which is no part of thee,
Take all myself.
2.2.47–49

I have night's cloak to hide me from their eyes,
And but thou love me, let them find me here.
My life were better ended by their hate
Than death prorogued, wanting of thy love.
2.2.75–78

By whose direction [did I find thee]?
By love, that first did prompt me to enquire.
He lent me counsel, and I lent him eyes.
2.2.79–81

I am no pilot, yet were thou as far
As that vast shore wash'd with the farthest sea,
I should adventure for such merchandise.

2.2.82–84

My bounty is as boundless as the sea,
My love as deep: the more I give to thee
The more I have, for both are infinite.

2.2.133–35

O blessed, blessed night. I am afeard,
Being in night, all this is but a dream,
Too flattering sweet to be substantial.

2.2.139–41

I [would] tear the cave where Echo lies
And make her airy tongue more hoarse than mine
With repetition of [your] name.

2.2.161–63

[When you speak] it is my soul that calls upon my
    name.

2.2.164

How silver-sweet sound lovers' tongues by night,
Like softest music to attending ears.

2.2.165–66

'Tis almost morning, I would have thee gone,
And yet no farther than a wanton's bird,
That lets it hop a little from his hand
Like a poor prisoner in his twisted gyves,
And with a silken thread plucks it back again,
So loving-jealous of his liberty.

2.2.176–81

Love's heralds should be thoughts
Which ten times faster glides than the sun's beams
Driving back shadows over lowering hills.

2.5.4–6

Come what sorrow can,
It cannot countervail the exchange of joy
That one short minute gives me in [your] sight.

2.6.3–5

[Let] love-devouring death do what he dare:
It is enough I may but call [you] mine.

2.6.7–8

The sweetest honey
Is loathsome in his own deliciousness,
And in the taste confounds the appetite.
Therefore love moderately; long love doth so.

2.6.11–14

If the measure of thy joy
Be heap'd like mine, and that thy skill be more
To blazon it, then sweeten with thy breath
This neighbour air, and let rich music's tongue
Unfold the imagin'd happiness that both
Receive in either by this dear encounter.

2.6.24–29

Come night, come [my love], come thou day in night,
For thou wilt lie upon the wings of night
Whiter than new snow upon a raven's back.

3.2.17–19

When [you] shall die
[May the night] take [you] and cut [you] out in little stars,
And [you] will make the face of heaven so fine

That all the world will be in love with night,
And pay no worship to the garish sun.

                              3.2.21–25

My bosom's lord sits lightly in his throne
And all this day an unaccustom'd spirit
Lifts me above the ground with cheerful thoughts.

                              5.1.3–5

Sweet flower, with flowers thy bridal bed I strew.

                              5.3.11

THE TAMING OF THE SHREW

[You] look as clear
As morning roses newly wash'd with dew.

                              2.1.172–73

Sweet dear, prove mistress of my heart.

                              4.2.10

Love wrought these miracles.

                              5.1.113

THE TEMPEST

These sweet thoughts do even refresh my labours.

                              3.1.14

Noble mistress; 'tis fresh morning with me
When you are by at night.

                              3.1.33–34

> By my modesty,
> The jewel in my dower, I would not wish
> Any companion in the world but you.
>
> 3.1.53–55

> O heaven, O earth, bear witness to this sound,
> And crown what I profess with kind event,
> If I speak true! if hollowly invert
> What best is boded me to mischief! I,
> Beyond all limit of what else i' th' world,
> Do love, prize, honour you.
>
> 3.1.68–73

> Fair encounter
> Of two most rare affections! Heavens rain grace
> On that which breeds between [us]!
>
> 3.1.74–76

> [Take me] as my gift, and thine own acquisition
> Worthily purchas'd.
>
> 4.1.13–14

> [I love you] dearly, my delicate.
>
> 4.1.49

> *Honour, riches, marriage-blessing,*
> *Long continuance, and increasing,*
> *Hourly joys be still upon you!*
>
> 4.1.106–8

> *Come temperate nymphs, and help to celebrate*
> *A contract of true love; be not too late.*
>
> 4.1.132–33

TROILUS AND CRESSIDA

Fair thoughts be your fair pillow.

3.1.44–45

Let thy song be love: this love will undo us all.

3.1.105

Ay, good now, love, love, nothing but love.

3.1.108

So dying love lives still.

3.1.119

[I am] in love, i'faith, to the very tip of the nose.

3.1.122

Sweet, above thought I love thee.

3.1.155

My heart beats thicker than a feverous pulse,
And all my powers do their bestowing lose,
Like vassalage at unawares encount'ring
The eye of majesty.

3.2.35–38

> But that the busy day,
Wak'd by the lark, hath rous'd the ribald crows,
And dreaming night will hide our joys no longer,
I would not from thee.

4.2.8–11

> I love thee in so strain'd a purity
That the blest gods, as angry with my fancy,
More bright in zeal than the devotion which
Cold lips blow to their deities, take thee from me.

4.4.23–26

Injurious Time now with a robber's haste
Crams his rich thiev'ry up, he knows not how;
As many farewells as be stars in heaven,
With distinct breath and consign'd kisses to them,
He fumbles up into a loose adieu,
and scants us with a single famish'd kiss
Distasted with the salt of broken tears.

$$4.4.41-47$$

Hear me, my love: be thou but true of heart.

$$4.4.57$$

She was belov'd, she lov'd; she is, and doth;
But still sweet love is food for fortune's tooth.

$$4.5.291-92$$

TWELFTH NIGHT

O spirit of love, how quick and fresh art thou!

$$1.1.9$$

[I love you]
With adorations, fertile tears,
With groans that thunder love, with sighs of fire.

$$1.5.260$$

But come what may, I do adore thee so,
That danger shall seem sport, and I will go.

$$2.1.46-47$$

O mistress mine, where are you roaming?
O stay and hear, your true love's coming,
That can sing both high and low.
Trip no further, pretty sweeting:

Journeys end in lovers meeting,
Every wise man's son doth know.

2.3.40–45

What is love? 'Tis not hereafter,
Present mirth hath present laughter:
What's to come is still unsure.
In delay there lies no plenty,
Then come kiss me, sweet and twenty:
Youth's a stuff will not endure.

2.3.48–53

If it be thus to dream, still let me sleep!

4.1.11

Now heaven walks on earth.

5.1.95

And all those sayings will I over-swear,
And all those swearings keep as true in soul
As doth that orbed continent the fire
That severs day from night.

5.1.267–70

When that is known, and golden time convents,
A solemn combination shall be made
Of our dear souls.

5.1.381–83

THE TWO GENTLEMEN OF VERONA

Sweet love, sweet lines, sweet life!
Here is [your] hand, the agent of [your] heart;
Here is [your] oath for love, [your] honour's pawn.

1.3.45–47

Alas, this parting strikes poor lovers dumb.

2.2.20

[You are] mine own,
And I as rich in having such a jewel
As twenty seas, if all their sand were pearl,
The water nectar, and the rocks pure gold.

2.4.164–67

O sweet-suggesting Love, if thou hast sinn'd,
Teach me (thy tempted subject) to excuse it.

2.6.7–8

Love, lend me wings to make my purpose swift
As thou hast lent me wit to plot this drift.

2.6.42–43

What light is light, if [you] be not seen?

3.1.174

What joy is joy, if [you] be not by?
Unless it be to think that [you are] by
And feed upon the shadow of perfection.

3.1.175–77

Except I be [beside you] in the night,
There is no music in the nightingale.
Unless I look [upon you] in the day,
There is no day for me to look upon.
[You are] my essence, and I leave to be,
If I be not by [your] fair influence
Foster'd, illumin'd, cherish'd, kept alive.

3.1.178–84

Who is Sylvia? What is she
That all our swains commend her?
Holy, fair, and wise is she,

The heaven such grace did lend her,
  That she might admired be.

Is she kind as she is fair?
For beauty lives with kindness.
Love doth to her eyes repair,
To help him of his blindness;
  And, being help'd, inhabits there.

Then to Sylvia let us sing,
That Sylvia is excelling;
She excels each mortal thing
Upon the dull earth dwelling.
  To her let us garlands bring.

4.2.38–52

THE WINTER'S TALE

[We] have seemed to be together, though absent; shook
  hands, as over a vast; and embraced, as it were, from
  the ends of opposed winds. The heavens continue
  [our] loves!

1.1.29–32

We [shall be] as twinn'd lambs that . . . frisk i' th' sun,
And bleat the one at th'other.

1.2.67–68

  They say we are
Almost as like as eggs.

1.2.129–30

[You're] all my exercise, my mirth, my matter:
Now my sworn friend, and then mine enemy;
My parasite, my soldier, statesman, all.

[You] make a July's day short as December;
And with [your] varying childness cure in me
Thoughts that would thick my blood.

1.2.166–71

I love you better . . . not for because
Your brows are blacker; yet black brows, they say,
Become some women best, so that there be not
Too much hair there, but in a semicircle,
Or a half-moon, made with a pen.

2.1.6–11

I'll be thine, my fair.

4.4.42

Lift up your countenance, as it were the day
Of celebration of that nuptial which
We two have sworn shall come.

4.4.49–51

What you do
Still betters what is done. When you speak, sweet,
I'd have you do it ever: when you sing,
I'd have you buy and sell so, so give alms,
Pray so, and, for the ord'ring your affairs,
To sing them too: when you do dance, I wish you
A wave o' th' sea, that you might ever do
Nothing but that, move still, still so,
And own no other function. Each your doing,
So singular in each particular,
Crowns what you are doing, in the present deeds,
That all your acts are queens.

4.4.135–46

Were I crown'd the most imperial monarch
Thereof most worthy, were I the fairest youth

That ever made eye swerve, had force and knowledge
More than was ever man's, I would not prize them
Without [your] love; for [you], employ them all;
Commend them and condemn them to [your] service,
Or to their own perdition.

4.4.373–79

Not for Bohemia, nor the pomp that may
Be thereat glean'd: for all the sun sees, or
The close earth wombs, or the profound seas hides
In unknown fathoms, will I break my oath
To [you] my fair belov'd.

4.4.489–93

    Dear, look up:
Though Fortune, visible an enemy,
Should chase us . . . power no jot
Hath she to change our loves.

5.1.215–17

ABOUT THE AUTHORS

Wayne F. Hill and Cynthia J. Öttchen are Americans living in England. While studying at Cambridge University, they came out of a performance of *Twelfth Night* laughing and trading insults they'd heard in the play. They found more ammunition in the text, then read another play, found more and more breathtaking invective, and at the end of the complete works were staring (still laughing) at almost 10,000 insults. They published about half of them, making Shakespeare's genius streetquotable as never before. With only word-of-mouth publicity, the rush of sales was so great that the London *Times* called it "a publishing miracle." Besieged by fans begging for more—"now please give us the other side of the coin"—Hill and Öttchen have turned their cocked eye to the language of seduction. Still amused, with over 120,000 suddenly more-literate readers behind them laughing too, they decided to launch *Shakespeare and the Art of Verbal Seduction* upon an unsuspecting world. What this will stimulate, they have no idea, and for it assume no responsibility.